It's Not About You

A Grandparent's Guide to Surviving Divorce in the Family

Jolyn Rudelson

Park East Press

Printed in the United States of America.

For information address:

Park East Press
The Graybar Building
420 Lexington Avenue, Suite 300
New York, NY 10170

Library of Congress Cataloging-in-Publication Data

Rudelson, Jolyn

It's Not About You/Jolyn Rudelson

Library of Congress Control Number: 2010937657

p. cm.

ISBN: 978-1-935764-17-5

10 9 8 7 6 5 4 3 2 1

To the Rudelson Men:

My son Jordan, who stood by me during some very difficult times;

My son Justin, who shared his most precious gifts with me;

My grandsons, Auden and Trillin, who fill my heart with joy;

And in memory of their grandfather, Jerrold (Jerry) Rudelson, who left me with a love that has lasted a lifetime.

It *is* all about you!

Acknowledgements

It's such a strange experience to write a book both as an observer and a participant. The difficult challenges presented while surviving divorce in my family were definitely expected. The rewards received after the first few years were not. I would like to acknowledge the members of my family who endured this with me.

My son, Dr. Justin Rudelson, whose amazing dignity through it all was a constant source of inspiration. My everlasting love for my grandsons, Auden and Trillin Rudelson, made writing this book well worth the effort. I hope that they will someday understand that in the writing of this book, the sacrifice they were called on to make at such an incredibly young age has been both acknowledged and appreciated. Special thanks to Auden Rudelson for taking the cover photo. And many thanks to my son, Jordan Rudelson, for all his efforts on my behalf. I couldn't have done this without his help.

I will always be grateful to my editor, Robert Middlemiss, for his patience, kindness and understanding to this first-time author. His incredible insight to the material helped me in so many ways. He was an inspiration.

Many thanks to my publisher, John Lewis, who believed that the subject of my book was important enough to be shared. At Park East Press I want to specifically thank Jennifer Adkins, copy editor, and Eric Lindsey, who designed the cover. Great job! A special thanks to my attorney, Joey Sayson, who took care of the legal details.

I really appreciate the emotional support and encouragement I received from my two closest friends, Helen Kozberg and Alizia Gur Schrager, and my dear friend and cousin-in-law, Martha Stevens. Also thanks to the unnamed friends and acquaintances whose stories are contained within these pages. Several of the stories concern late members of my family whom I would like to remember:

my father and mother, William and Hilda Feinblum, and my sister, Sandra Tobin.

My late husband, Jerry Rudelson, deserves special thanks for his important contribution to this book. It was because of my life as the wife of an adult child of divorce I was able to appreciate the challenges involved. And last but not least, to all the grandparents who have been called on to survive divorce in their families, I wish you and your families a successful divorce.

Table of Contents

Rule One

It's Not About You!

I have been forced to deal with three devastating events in my life. The first was when my husband was killed in a plane crash. I was 38, mother of two sons, ten and almost thirteen, and in an instant, a widow. The second came when I was sixty-seven and received the dreaded news: I had cancer. The third struck after I had become a grandmother of two grandsons, just two and a half and almost four, and my son announced he was getting a divorce. Each of these proved life altering, each required a journey of education, and each required survival.

I was sixty-eight the first time the title of grandparent was bestowed on me. My son called to tell me my first grandson had arrived. What was so amazing to me was that I had done absolutely nothing, but I had just received the best title of my life: grandmother. Or as I had pre-selected, "Grandy," from a favorite novel. At that minute I knew I would be happy to spend the rest of my life earning the right to the name. The fact that my grandson had been delivered in a huge, warm pool of water should have been my first clue that the world had indeed changed. My husband hadn't even been allowed in the delivery room when this baby's daddy was born, but my son was allowed to share in it all.

How I wished I wasn't three thousand miles away when he was born! But after the mastectomy, chemo had left this new grandmother wheelchair bound, in the middle of physical therapy sessions that would finally get me back on my feet. Yet the timing couldn't have been better. Watching my grandchild's growth, even from a distance, would be a lot more fun than worrying about my life expectancy, or dealing with the usual health issues that were occurring with aging.

A year and a half later, another precious water-born grandson was added to our family. A picture of him, just a few minutes old, on my computer the same day, again reminded me how the world was moving forward. The stability of my younger child's marriage, with two happy and healthy grandchildren, certainly contributed to my great feeling of well-being, adding a great deal of focus to my life. No wonder, two and a half years later, those three little words, "We're getting divorced," so rocked my world, just like it does for any grandparent.

Eventually, I would have to acknowledge that with my son's announcement of "THE DIVORCE," I had just been issued a warning; a bomb was about to explode in the middle of my family. If I had really been honest with myself, I would have admitted to having felt a few pre-warning tremors. You know. Those warning signals. The chill that goes up the middle of your back when you are around your child's family and catch a look, a shrug, an angry tone, or even a muffled conversation overheard on the phone. No, it turned out I had not imagined something was wrong. Something was.

I immediately made the first mistake every parent makes whose child has just announced a divorce. I started to fight for time: "Oh, it can't possibly be as bad as you think! Maybe if you sleep on it, the situation won't look as unsolvable to you in the morning," or "Don't you think you should both try counseling before you consider such a drastic step?" Yes, I admit it. I did all of that and then some, getting the expected response of "Moooother, don't you think I already tried all that before calling you with the news?" I could see his eyes rolling even from so far away.

I got off the phone, the old phrase left over from my World War II childhood running through my head. It reminded me of my teacher issuing the drill, "Prepare to duck and cover," as we were sent ducking under our desks to avoid the impending atomic blast. Instead of a desk, I found myself tucking myself into my bed, curled into a fetal position for several days, trying to avoid the emotional fragments.

Too early in life I learned the lesson that survival is a natural instinct. But how well we survive requires acceptance and education. The more we know, the less we fear. When I dealt with widowhood and breast cancer, I was forced to focus on myself, but this time focusing on myself didn't seem to be working. I just couldn't get myself out of bed. At first my thoughts kept going to my grandchildren, only two and a half and almost four. How were they going to deal with the loss of their father in the home? What was going to happen to my child, being separated from his children? Then, regardless of how hard it was for me to admit it, the hardest of all for me to face, was the nagging thought that welled up inside my head, emerging in a silent scream: "What about MEEEEEE????????"

I had just had my first flash of awareness. Grandparents, along with their grandchildren, are very much a part of the collateral damage of the divorce. The only difference is they are the *unacknowledged* victims of divorce in the family. Just like the title of Grandmother that had come unearned, I was going to be forced to deal with the unbidden repercussions from the divorce.

After wallowing in that knowledge for several days, all the while feeling extremely sorry for myself, those familiar survival instincts began to kick in. It was during my first attempts to figure out how I could work to survive this that I had a major epiphany: regardless of how badly the divorce was going to impact me, it suddenly hit me. *It's not about you!* Also, I realized, I could not realistically expect any comfort to come from any members of my own family. They were dealing with their own pain. Even professionals, so used to focusing on helping the divorcing couple and their children, might not be so helpful. As an unacknowledged victim of divorce, I would just have to find a way to help myself.

That realization, *It's not about you*, focused my attention in an entirely different direction. Instead of my survival being first and foremost, this time my goal had to be finding a way to help my child and grandchildren survive the divorce with the least possible harm. In order to accomplish that, I was first going to have to educate myself on what was ahead for all of us.

I have always thought education starts with books, so I was frustrated to find that there was not one book that would answer my questions on how a grandparent could survive divorce in the family. Instead it was going to take a lot of research to find the information I needed, as well as my experiencing the problems, before the answers were clear. I was going to have to find a way to be helpful to those I love without being intrusive, and helping those I love would have to be the way I would help myself, as well.

The first thing I came to realize early in my search for information is that, like snowflakes, no two divorces are alike. The reasons for the divorce can seem similar, but the personalities of the two parties involved make each situation different. The families they bring into and out of the marriage are different. And certainly the children involved can differ in age, gender and number. But just as divorces differ, there remains a commonality of problems and situations that are the same.

Now, one grandparent to another, I offer you this guide. It carries the results of that educational journey I have been on during the first six years of my family's divorce. I hope that sharing the ten rules I learned will help you cross the minefield you are about to enter, that you will proceed uninjured, and that you will avoid adding any additional injuries to those you love along the way.

At first each grandparent may think he or she is all alone in this conflict. But you have a lot of company, even royal company. "*Annus horribles*," Queen Elizabeth II proclaimed when Prince Charles got divorced, the Queen Mother died and Windsor Castle burned. That was the way the queen described the royal family's year of 1992.

You may not be your country's monarch, but it is not surprising if you feel just like the queen did. Your castle is crumbling. Let's face it—it is very comforting to find out that other families, even royal ones, have their horrible years too. Your own horrible year is just about to begin, so buckle up for the bumpy ride ahead. But try at all costs to keep your sense of humor. You are going to need it.

First, don't beat yourself up if, when your child dropped the divorce bomb, you responded with the same insensitive questions I did. You were just fighting for time to get over the shock you were in. Now that you are aware of the trouble an insensitive mouth can get you, just don't repeat it.

Preparedness is the best protection against the shock waves that have hit you. I am not suggesting you stockpile extra supplies of water and canned goods, but for those late evening, unexpected visits from your child, you might want to have some comfort food waiting in the freezer, and of course, Kleenex. If a drop-in is unlikely because of the distance involved, you always have the phone and e-mail to keep you close, and the comfort food can be for you.

When the separation occurs, it will be like an earthquake. One minute you are standing on firm ground, and the next minute your family foundation will start to crack, eventually splitting down the middle. The divorce in the family will affect everyone. Each person's life, including yours, will be shaken to the core.

Marriage, it appears, can be a temporary institution. But divorce is forever. With the divorce, your child will get a new title or number, like first or second husband or wife. But *your* grandparent title, once received, will never change. By no act of your own, you were created a grandparent. And like it or not, by no act of your own, you are part of the divorce in progress.

When the shock starts to fade and you begin to face the emotional ramifications of your child's divorce, your first concern will instinctively be your grandchildren. You will be forced to face the fact that the divorce will have a profound effect on them. The extent of this will be unknown for some time. The fact that your grandchildren will no longer have the benefit of a two-parent household will probably hit you hard. This is what I dwelled on in the beginning. After my husband died, I had the experience of being a single parent. It wasn't easy. I understood just how difficult it would be for my grandchildren, and how the effects of the divorce could last well into their adulthood.

There will be so many unanswered questions. You will keep asking yourself: how often will you get to see and talk to your grandchildren? Will you ever celebrate birthdays and holidays as a family again, or all those other milestone times all grandparents look forward to, like graduations, weddings or religious ceremonies marking the growing up of our grandchildren? The answers to some of them will work themselves out in the coming months and years. So don't dwell on them now.

Next you will be thinking about the challenging readjustments your child is going to be forced to deal with. If you have a daughter, the thought of her raising her children alone, dealing with finances, child support, childcare, housing, and possibly a job search, will seem overwhelming. If you have a son, the hard realization that two really could live as cheaply as one, but that maintaining Mommy's House and Daddy's House is a very expensive proposition, may make you worry about how your son will be able to manage all that extra expense. It may have the *déjà vu* aspect of his single days, while making you wonder if he has considered that when his children are with him, there will literally be little mouths to feed, clothe and keep entertained. And even more demanding, with teenagers, what to do when they would rather spend their time with their friends than their fathers?

Those sacred wedding vows, "For better or worse, for richer, for poorer, in sickness and in health," that are ended for the parents at the time of their divorce turn out to be sacred vows after all. They are everlasting between parent and child.

Also, if you considered your child's spouse as one of your children, you will end up feeling like you have just lost a child. You will experience the grieving process that follows. I felt that tremendous sense of loss myself. My daughter-in-law and I had become very close during the time she had been married to my son. I could never forget that when I went into the hospital to have my cancer surgery, she moved into my hospital room for four days to make sure I got the proper care. How do you recover the loss of a bond like that?

Divorce will impact the total family on generational levels. As grandparents, you face the uncertainty of your future, just as your child and grandchildren face the uncertainty of theirs. Is it selfish for you to worry about how your child's divorce will affect the rest of your life? Not really. It is the fear of the unknown. Grandparents are overlooked as victims of the family's divorce, so it is only natural to indulge your "What about me?" frame of mind. You definitely deserve some time to get your emotions in check.

There is one major problem for all grandparents. It is unrealistic to expect too much comfort from your own family. You can't go to your child. He or she is suffering enough. Nor can you go to your grandchildren, even if they are older. They have their own problems to deal with. It will also be difficult to seek comfort from friends. Many of them will have already gone through a divorce in their own family. (Remember that fifty-percent statistic.) You are going to have to handle this survival on your own, unless you seek out professional help. And they may not be too sympathetic. "It's not about you," after all. It's all right to take a little time to feel sorry for yourself, but sorrow, you will find, is a luxury you can't afford.

All right, I said you could take some time to deal with the shock from the divorce announcement. But it has to be short. Cancel your pity party. No one will accept the invitation. They are engaged elsewhere. You will find out quickly that nobody but you is losing sleep about your adjustment to your child's divorce. Eventually—the sooner the better—I hope you too will have the sudden epiphany I had, that your child's divorce impacts you, but IT'S

NOT ABOUT YOU. And your family needs you to help them cope.

When you finally get to this point of removing the "you" out of the divorce equation, you are ready to start your education. When you understand what the divorce action will involve, you will be ready to help your child and grandchildren get through the times ahead. Preparing myself for what's to come is what has helped me survive so far. But what I've learned is that adjustment to divorce is a work in progress.

For you grandmothers and grandfathers who are already reading this book, you probably are on your third pizza or pan of lasagna, and you've consumed a quart of rocky road, the flavor of divorce. You've reached out for some helpful books from your neighborhood library, or the bookstore perhaps, or if you are a "with it" grandparent, the Internet. Your preparation and education for your family's survival have begun. What follows are the Ten Rules I discovered that you can use to survive your own divorce in the family. They are helping me to survive mine. I hope they will assist you with your own adjustment. I hope they will guide you in aiding your family to get through theirs.

Rule One:
It's Not About You

Rule Two:

Your Day Is Done

The first thing I did when I finally got myself functioning after my son dropped the divorce bomb was to research information to help me understand what the modern twenty-first century divorce is like. The facts and data were accessible, but not in one place. Like a mosaic, the picture of divorce began to come together. Divorce had definitely changed since my day, and I bet since yours too.

During those first conversations with my son, I heard myself saying "In my day" too many times. Even my eyes were rolling. It didn't take me long to find out "my day" had long passed. It made me laugh when I realized "my day" was now consigned to the pages of cultural history. Hard as it may be, old as it may make you feel, you are going to have to put your day behind you, as I did. And you must accept the changes to marriage and divorce that have occurred since you said your "I Do's."

Once I familiarized myself with the modern-day language of divorce, I found it so much easier to have meaningful conversations with my son. Learning these terms will help you too, especially in those first emotionally-charged discussions you'll have with your child. It's a good place to start in understanding the modern-day divorce.

The Language of Divorce

DIVORCE: The legal ending (dissolution) of a marriage.

FAULT DIVORCE: One spouse charging the other with a type of

legal misconduct (grounds) in order to be granted a divorce from the other. Legal grounds in most states consist of adultery, abandonment, abuse, incurable insanity, imprisonment, drug and/or alcohol addiction.

NO-FAULT DIVORCE: Proof of misconduct is no longer necessary. Grounds for granting a divorce consist of less confrontational terms: irreconcilable differences, incompatibility or the irretrievable breakdown of the marriage.

IRRECONCILABLE DIFFERENCES: One or both spouses in a marriage are no longer able or willing to continue in a marriage relationship. Also referred to as an "irretrievable breakdown of marriage."

COLLABORATIVE DIVORCE: This is an out-of court type of divorce practiced by an organization of attorneys. Their goal is to provide a faster, more affordable method of obtaining a divorce. The goal is to minimize the hostility between the couple seeking divorce. The attorney for each side supports the two spouses in reaching a mutual decision regarding the division of their property, spousal and child support, and custody issues concerning the children of the divorce. If the couple fails to reach a decision on any of these issues, resulting in the need for litigation, this type of attorney will withdraw from representation, unless he or she also practices divorce litigation.

DIVORCE (FAMILY) COURT: State court assigned to handle all issues relating to families: divorce, support, custody, guardianship adoption, and issuing of restraining orders concerning domestic violence.

DIVORCE DECREE: The legal document issued by the court which officially ends the marriage as of a specified date.

DIVORCED: The period after a marriage has officially been terminated which, regardless of the re-marriage of either spouse, continues until their death. The effects of this period also impact all the other members of the family, including the children of the divorce and their grandparents.

Types of Support:

SPOUSAL SUPPORT OR ALIMONY: Monthly payments, determined by court order or settlement, paid by one divorced spouse to the other. This support, usually paid by the former husband to the wife for a set period of time, allows the spouse needing the support time to retrain or obtain employment in order to become self-supporting. "Spousal support" is the newer term used in no-fault and collaborative divorces instead of "alimony." The length of time this support is awarded is based upon the duration of the marriage and the age and physical condition of the spouse.

CHILD SUPPORT: Monthly court-ordered or approved payments paid by the non-custodial parent to the custodial parent for support of the children of the marriage until their majority. These payments are determined by state guidelines contained in a Child Support Obligation Schedule. The combined monthly net incomes of both parents are considered in determining the monthly child support payment required of the non-custodial parent.

Custody:

PHYSICAL CUSTODY: The right granted to a parent to have the child(ren) reside with father or mother either exclusively (sole custody) or shared (joint custody) for a specified time with each parent during the year, also called "co-parenting." A rarer form of joint custody is called "bird nesting." In this type of custody, the children remain in the family home. The parents alternately move in and out on a set Parenting Time Schedule, each maintaining another residence when they are not with the children.

CUSTODIAL PARENT: The parent who resides with the

child(ren) for the major part of the year, usually the mother, is termed the custodial parent. The other parent is referred to as the non-custodial or non-residential parent.

PARENTING PLAN: A schedule set up by the parents, with court approval, usually a year in advance, determining which parent has physical custody of the child(ren) on dates specified. The time each parent is scheduled to have the child(ren) reside with them is referred to as "parenting time."

LEGAL CUSTODY: The right and responsibility to make all important decisions regarding a child of divorce's welfare: ie, education, health, religion, etc. This type of custody is awarded equally to both parents in the case of joint custody, but to only one parent or caregiver in the case of sole custody.

GUARDIAN AD LITEM (GAL): A court-appointed representative to protect the interests of a minor child in divorcing or divorced families. A GAL may be appointed when the parents are not willing or able to come to agreement with regard to decisions affecting their child(ren)'s welfare, requiring the intervention of the court system to make those decisions and ensure that they are carried out.

Types of Families

NUCLEAR FAMILY: An "Ozzie & Harriet" type of family consisting of mother, father and their natural or adopted children. There now also exists a same-sex nuclear family in which there are two parents of the same sex raising either the natural child of one parent or the adopted child of one or both parents.

EXTENDED FAMILY: Members of a nuclear family plus the grandparents, siblings and their children, with some either living separately or under the same roof.

BINUCLEAR FAMILY: "Mommy's House and Daddy's House": the two halves of a child of divorce's life. This type of family also can consist of spouses of one or both parents after remarriage.

STEPPARENT: The new spouse of a parent, with no legal rights granted regarding that parent's children as a result of this remarriage.

BLENDED FAMILY: A family that consists of child(ren) from one or both spouses' previous marriage(s) as well as any children who are offspring of the current marriage.

MIX-MASTER FAMILY: A family which consists of children from each of the spouse's former marriage(s), whether living there full time or living with their other parent part of the time, plus natural children they share. These families are made up of members that are not necessarily together at the same time, but whose makeup changes depending on the children's schedules with the other parent. Also, the parents and children involved in these families can change depending on the length of the marriages controlling the mix.

GPG FAMILY: A family where a maternal or paternal grandparent has the court-appointed role of parent for his or her grandchildren. It occurs in most cases due to the death, incapacity, or incarceration of either or both parents.

PARENTAL ALIENATION: Any continual action by one parent which prevents the other parent from exercising his or her right to maintain a relationship with his or her child after a divorce.

Okay, if you've managed to wade through these terms, the next step on your journey of understanding is finding out why it was necessary to create them.

Till Divorce Do We Part

At the very beginning of my search for information, I found that since I had married over fifty years ago, marriage and divorce had changed. It was a new playing field, sometimes constructive but now often difficult and perhaps vindictive. The words of Robert Browning that my husband would recite to me every anniversary kept running through my mind: "Grow old along with me; the best is yet to be…" It filled me with sadness that due to all the changes in marriage, my son and grandsons might never know the joy of sharing a love that lasts a lifetime.

I kept asking myself, where was I when the wedding vows were changed from "Till death do us part" to "Till divorce do us part"? Boredom now seems as valid a ground for divorce as irreconcilable differences. It seems to me that marriage these days appears to be only for providing legitimacy to the offspring of the union. Once legitimatized, these children are too often seen as secondary to the fulfillment of their parents' other needs.

Regardless of how much time has elapsed since your marriage, or divorce, the changes probably are surprising, even alarming, to you too. Unless your divorce was just a year or two ago, you will find that only the pain remains the same.

Expiration Date of Marriage

The more I looked into divorce, the more it seemed that marriage comes with an expiration date, just like food in my refrigerator. If the published reports are correct, fifty percent of first marriages, sixty percent of second marriages and seventy percent of third marriages end in divorce. The hardest part of the increased rate of divorce is that those divorces involve a million children annually. As if that wasn't bad enough, half of the children of the first divorce will live to be a victim of one, or both, of the failures of their parents' second marriages. Ten percent of those same children will be part of three or more breakups.

For some, marriage does not get any better with practice. Once a parent runs from marriage the first time, it seems, it is much easier to run from the second, or more. Maybe there should be some limitations on the number of marriages allowed. Treat them like a privilege instead of a right. It could be like getting a driver's license. You need to take some kind of test to get one. Then if you have enough serious accidents (divorces) with multiple injuries (children and exes), your privilege to get a license could be revoked permanently. If that is unreasonable, how about requiring a yearlong course on marriage and relationships? Before permitting people to be in a position to inflict further damage on their children, have them study what is required for a successful marriage and divorce.

What is so amazing, with the fifty-fifty odds of a marriage being everlasting, is that newlyweds still take their vows. They still have "happily ever after" expectations of marriage. Even though the roles of women have been changing, women are still pursuing the fairy tale. They don't accept the fact that making a marriage work is not the sole responsibility of the white knight. Their knight may have ridden into the marriage astride his horse, but the wife needs to have a shovel ready to clean up the droppings.

Marriage is no longer like the old teeter-totter of our childhood, with the lighter of the pair left in the air, depending on the stronger one to bring her safely to the ground. The modern-day marriage depends on equality between the sexes, each partner carrying sixty percent of the responsibilities for the other.

Couples seem to expect more from marriage these days. But they are not willing to work at their marriages long enough to realize those expectations. They "try out" marriage like they try on a pair of shoes, something to be returned at the first sign of blisters.

I was confused by all the data that turned up. I kept remembering many of my friends trying to work out their problems, not run away from them. Or at the very least, they delayed divorce until the children grew up, graduated high school, and/or left for college. Several of my friends' husbands even waited to exit the closet until their children were old enough to deal with it.

Forty years ago, ninety percent of children were reared to maturity by married, natural parents. In the early seventies the number of children living with both parents started to decline, until by

1996 it had reached sixty-eight percent. The consequence? More children are being forced to live in single-parent families as a result of divorce, even more than those children being born to teenage mothers.

The more information started to build up in my divorce research file, the more I began to question whether all the changes to marriage and divorce were for the better. But as a grandparent, I knew I had better keep that opinion to myself. You, too, will find yourself grappling with thoughts like this in the coming months. If you are like me, you'll find it best to keep a lot of views to yourself.

All right, grandparents, it's time to face the music. Those very same parents that waited to get their divorces until the children grew up are the grandfathers and grandmothers of today. The number of grandparents without a divorce in their past is decreasing, as the divorce rate in the senior citizen age group is on the rise as well. As people live longer and healthier lives, widowed grandparents are choosing a last grab for the brass ring. As unhappily married seniors see their life span increase, an opportunity might present itself to seek a final shot at happiness. Many more seniors' marriages are ending by divorce instead of death.

According to Dr. Merril Silverstein, a professor at the USC Davis School of Gerontology, almost half of the families with children have at least one set of grandparents who have been divorced, compared with one-fifth of families with children in the mid-1980s. It appears to show a trend that a good percentage of children of divorce are not only being forced to deal with their own parents' divorce but the effect of their grandparents' divorce as well. And children of nuclear families will also be feeling the effects of divorce in their family.

Grandchildren can be affected almost as much by their grandparents' divorce as by their own parents'. When grandparents divorce, there is a deep disruption of family stability. Since a grandfather's relationship with his grandchildren has proven, in many cases, to be diminished by a divorce from the grandmother, the security the grandchildren have been looking to their grandparents to provide them after their own parents divorced will no longer be available.

Remember when monogamy was expected in marriage? Infidelity by the husband caused waves of gossip through a neighborhood. But committed by the wife? This proved to be a major scandal. By 1992 a survey by the National Opinion Research Center of the University of Chicago found 65% of marriages ended because of adultery by one or both spouses. Many divorces nowadays result from the wife's infidelity, one by-product of the women's lib movement. And some divorces result not because of the husband's infidelities with "the other woman," or even the wife's infidelity with another man, but rather from a same-sex relationship. Both the women's lib movement and the assertion of gay rights have caused married men and women to rethink how they wish to live.

It seems that monogamous relationships are now only left to some of the animal species, like bald eagles, gray wolves, swans and, of course, the symbol of marriage, the lovebird. Even the animal kingdom is having a problem with monogamy, with only three percent of mammals considered monogamous, and of course, that doesn't include humans. For the animals that live in pairs but fool around, scientists have even coined the term "social monogamy." Come to think of it, that term could be applied to many of our still-married couples. For the marriage repeaters in the human species, the modern descriptive term is "serial monogamy." Although for those marrying for the third time or more, the term "sequential polygamy" might be more appropriate.

Several social changes led to the dramatic rise of divorces in the United States. They started in the mid-sixties. Prior to the 1960's, divorce was not that well accepted. Divorcing couples risked ostracism by their friends and families. At that time the end of a marriage could only be obtained by charges of the "Triple As," adultery, abuse or abandonment, that one spouse committed against the other. Many couples felt forced to commit perjury by admitting to the accepted grounds for divorce, even if untrue. Also at that time, a spouse who refused to agree to a divorce could hold the other spouse in the marriage against his or her will.

Ozzie and Harriet, Adieu, Adios and Goodbye!

The overcrowding of colleges caused by the influx of World War II and Korean War veterans attending under the 1944 G.I. Bill of Rights eased by the time the original G.I. Bill ended in 1956. As space became available, women started to go to college in greater numbers to get more than an "MRS" degree. A lot of these women, however, put off the use of their newly obtained educational credentials. They opted instead for the traditional role of wife and mother that the society of the time expected. They held the Mrs. degree by default.

I must admit I was one of them. When I entered UCLA Law School in 1954, our professor told us to look around at the other 99 students in the room because only half of us would make it to graduation. I didn't think it at all strange that of those looking back at me, only twelve were women. I made it to graduation all right, but only to cheer on my new husband as he got his law degree. We were the first couple to meet and marry in the law school. Most of the other women in the class not only graduated, but followed our example and married fellow classmates.

In the beginning of the 1960s, the "Ozzie and Harriet" picture of marriage started to erode. It was a book called *The Feminine Mystique*, written by Betty Friedan in 1963, that really started to shake things up. She identified the feelings that women were experiencing that something was lacking in their lives as "the problem with no name." Friedan pointed out that the idealized image of femininity, which she coined the "Feminine Mystique," denies women the opportunity to develop their own identities.

Books and articles by the likes of activists Gloria Steinem and Germaine Greer followed with a similar theme, which gave rise to ever-growing meetings of dissatisfied women. The strains of Peggy Lee singing "Is That All There Is?" in 1969 were replaced with a more strident rendition of Helen Reddy's "I Am Woman" in 1972.

With the trend toward smaller families, women were young enough when the empty nest syndrome started to kick in to take advantage of the increasing number of employment opportunities. This led to a changing family picture as many wives and mothers moved into the work force. Do these women sound familiar? They should; they are the grandmothers of today.

The economic opportunities that started to present themselves for women came with choices and confusion. Did joining the work force mean sacrificing their old goals of wife and mother? Was it possible to have it all—happy marriage, independent income, the feeling of accomplishment?

The rise in the divorce rate at that time would seem to indicate wives and mothers had not yet figured that out. Women, for the first time, could bring home the bacon, and if their husbands were not helpful, they could also "fry it in the pan." The higher the woman's income in relation to the family's total income, the more likely she was to look to divorce as the solution to an unhappy marriage, and the less likely she was to stay and make it work.

In the 1960s women were longing for fulfillment… if only they knew what that was. The juggling that was required between employee and homemaker proved to be much more difficult than they had anticipated. For many it was too late. Once they opted for a paycheck, there was no turning back.

Women's Lib and Its Costs

As women brought home their own paychecks, there developed growing unrest. Women started to compete for jobs with their male counterparts, but their recognition that they were being paid unequally began to create a major resentment between the working sexes. The women had only to look at the separate job listings for men and women in the want ads of the fifties and sixties to become aware of the inequities.

Even the slow-to-act government took notice that women were only receiving 59% of the pay men were receiving. The passage of the 1963 Equal Pay Act made it illegal to pay women lower rates for the same job strictly on the basis of their sex. It certainly looked good on paper, but it has taken much longer to accomplish. By 2008 it had only reached 77%.

The founding of the National Women's Political Caucus in 1971 by Betty Friedan, Gloria Steinem, Bella Abzug and Shirley Chisholm, among others, was the beginning of other feminist organizations developing around the world. Once the media took note, the story of the women's lib movement began to spread throughout the globe, fifty-two years after the 19th Amendment affirming women's right to vote was ratified in 1920.

In the "second wave" for women's rights, women's political groups worked to get an Equal Rights Amendment passed. Finally they felt they had a victory when on March 22, 1972, the proposed 27th Amendment to the Constitution passed both houses of Congress and was sent to the states with a seven-year deadline placed on the ratification process. "Equality of rights under the law shall not be denied or abridged by the United States or by any state on account of sex" required ratification by three-fourths of the states (38) to become part of the Constitution.

Pro-ERA groups led by the National Organization for Women did not let down on their efforts to get the law passed. But they had not expected to hit the brick wall that was erected successfully by such opposition groups as The Eagle Forum/STOP ERA group led by right-wing leader Phyllis Schlafly. As reasons to prevent the ratification of the Equal Rights Amendment, old fears were raised, among them that women would be sent into combat, abortion rights and homosexual marriages would be upheld, women would be denied the right to alimony from their husbands at the time of the divorce.

Even though the ratification deadline was extended to 1982, ratification of the ERA has been successfully prevented to this day. It looked like Schlafly, the Eagle Forum and the other conservatives who supported the defeat of the ERA had won the battle. But on closer inspection, it appears that they lost the war.

The very fears they raised as reasons to prevent ratification were not, it seems, fears of the majority. There are women on the front lines of the military, same sex marriages are law in some states, abortion rights are granted under the law, and the right to alimony has been limited. We have had female secretaries of state, senators, representatives, Supreme Court justices, governors, and even ministers and rabbis. It seems that changes affecting women's equality occurred without any law to allow them.

In the seventies and eighties, women tried to have it all: marriage, children, and employment. I was widowed and raising two sons during this period, and it was the hardest thing I have ever done.

Women began to take sides. On one side were women who felt they had a right to equality and wanted to seek the opportunities provided. On the other side, many were satisfied with the status quo. "Why," demanded Schlafly, "should women lower themselves to equal rights when we already have the status of special privilege?" This position was expressed by the joke of the time, "Why in the world would we want to stoop to equality?"

It was a grandiose claim that ignored the growing number of divorced or single parents—or rather, it erased the knowledge of their existence. Those women enjoyed being asked out a week in advance, having their car doors opened, and being taken out to dinner on the gentleman's dollar. You know, the old-fashioned, flowers-and-candy, genteel courting of their grandparents' day. That group was more interested in concentrating on being feminine than in taking on Feminism.

While many women were focusing on their goal of equality and all the benefits they would acquire, the men who at first had felt their masculinity being threatened started looking at the social and economic advantages that were developing for them. It could first be seen in the changes that took place at work. If women wanted equality, they would get it. But it would be through the slow erosion of their special female work perks.

Women working late in the evening were no longer provided dinner vouchers, escorts into those dark parking garages, or cab fare to get them home safe and sound. And lest we forget, there was the slow disappearance of those special rooms businesses were required to provide, with a bed where women employees rested during those special days of the month. Of course, the men employees missed those too, having used them, before the days of accusations about sexual harassment, for their assignations with female employees.

The Gift of Equality: The No-Fault Divorce

A change in divorce law was not exactly one of the goals of the Women's Movement, but it had that unexpected result. A backlash or fallout of sorts occurred called no-fault divorce. It started in California in 1969, when twice-married Governor Ronald Reagan signed into law the newly passed Family Law Act. The new law, called no-fault divorce, replaced the old common law action for divorce with dissolution of marriage. The new grounds, "irreconcilable differences," covered it all: adultery, abuse, abandonment, and of course, the increasing favorite reason, boredom. What could be better than taking the blame out of divorce, removing the pain of fault and burden for both men and women? Could a law be more equal?

No-fault may have begun in California, but by 1985 the new law had swept across the country and been adopted everywhere. The initial effect of the no-fault divorce could have been expected. During the seventies, the divorce rate doubled. Even though married couples in their twenties comprised only twenty percent of the population, they contributed to sixty percent of the couples divorcing in the sixties and seventies. It was almost as if the adoption of no-fault divorce gave tacit social acceptance to divorce, previously odious and suggesting shame and failure. It is the old chicken and the egg principle. Did no-fault divorce change the way society looked at divorce? Or had the change in society's perception of divorce created the climate that allowed it to be adopted?

Of course, not all of the increase in divorces could be laid at the new law's doorstep. But a 1989 study by lawyer and sociologist Thomas B. Marvell, "Divorce Rates and the Fault Requirement," concluded that divorces, on average, increased by some twenty to twenty-five percent as a result of the divorce law change, especially for couples with children. Once the law was changed, couples who had previously felt imprisoned by the old fault system acted fast. Husbands and wives in marginal marriages, who still found themselves looking for that greener pasture just over the nearest hill, decided no-fault gave them the chance to get out of their marriage to try for happiness in their next one. This period was called the Divorce Boom. It was the fastest-growing marital status of the times.

An interesting result of no-fault divorce was that wives seemed to be getting less from no-fault than their husbands. The greatest loss to women, at the same time as they were achieving increasing gains in equality, was the change in alimony and child support. Awarding alimony to a spouse at the end of the marriage for an unlimited period was no longer considered their right.

Since no-fault divorce was adopted, the term "alimony" has been changed. Now referred to as "spousal support," it is considered on a case-to-case basis. It takes into consideration the age, health, and educational level of the spouse and the length of the couple's marriage. Only about fifteen percent of divorced spouses are considered eligible. Some spouses are awarded alimony for a limited time to allow them to obtain education or job training to become self-supporting. Child support was also restructured.

Women are now required to start contributing equally to their children's support from their working income.

Of course, older women, usually over fifty and after long marriages, were still given alimony. They were considered—rather brutally, but with some job-market truth—too old to retrain. It's also interesting that by the time no-fault was adopted, the AARP, created in 1958 and devoted to the needs of people fifty and older, was in a position to expand their role and exercise their newfound power.

Who's Minding the Home Fires?

The biggest changes wrought in the last forty years affecting marriage and divorce have been among women. Is it that some women now consider marriage solely as their ticking biological clock solution, and after the child-bearing period is over and the work of bringing up children starts to ease, the marriage ends? Or is it that the ticking of the clock may force women into less stable marriages? In and out again, as soon as the clock has wound down and the crib is filled?

With some women there is a growing theme that fathers are becoming optional—an accessory, not a necessity. Those women view fathers as technically unnecessary, sidestepped biologically as more pregnancies are begun in the laboratory rather than in the bedroom. Some women consider in-vitro or artificial insemination from a sperm bank a viable alternative to become pregnant. Why marry at all? It seems that no less than the British House of Commons agreed with this position in June of 2008, when they rejected legislation which included a clause requiring a fertility doctor "to consider a child's need for a male role model before giving women IVF treatment."

We live in a time of disposable marriages. Our idealistic bonding, represented by the romanticism of the forties, is being jettisoned along with disposable appliances, cell phones, obsolete computers and clunker cars. They are cheaper to replace then to repair.

24

Some wives seem to feel the new kind of "try it on for size" marriage is normal. And since fifty-five percent of husbands and wives both work, the stay-at-home mother is fast becoming a thing of the past, going the way of Betamax video tape, TV picture tubes and full leaded gasoline. In its place the number of fathers who have taken on the stay at home child-care role, replacing wives who are earning more, is on the increase.

Working wives feel they are contributing as much to the support of the family as their husbands. They can support themselves and don't feel forced to stay in an unhappy marriage in order to feed their children. Since employed mothers are making their own contributions to Social Security, there is no reason to wait around for the obligatory ten years of marriage to qualify for their husband's benefits. They proceed to the divorce court.

No-fault by itself was still not considered to be enough for the divorce-minded. As more and more divorces began to be initiated by wives, women weren't just satisfied with the legal finding of no-fault. Now they wanted their divorces to be no-fault socially, as well. Their goal was divorce on demand, guilt free, fast, and inexpensive.

The Warm and Fuzzy Divorce

It took twenty years of working toward a "good divorce" to finally lead a Minnesota family attorney, Stuart Webb, to work out a new concept in 1990 called the "collaborative divorce." It was this term more than any other that my son mentioned in those first few days after dropping the "D" bomb, which pointed out my need to catch up quickly on how marriage and divorce had changed. Several of his friends suggested this type of divorce as the one they took advantage of because it was more economical than any other. My first suggestion, as his mother and widow of an attorney, was for him to wait on making any decision until he was up to speed on how his rights would be protected under this type of representation.

Looking into it, we found out that the concept was indeed revolutionary: attorneys working with each other instead of against each other to achieve a non-adversarial, out-of-court divorce. The initial focus was simple: to help families restructure, with the least expense, the smallest amount of emotional damage, and the best possible interest of the children as the primary goals. It developed a whole new field of lawyers in the practice of divorce law across the country, attorneys now working to practice family law without bitterness and hostility developing between the couple. It is referred to as the ADR approach (Alternate Dispute Resolution), for couples who would rather obtain their divorce peacefully, without having to go to court.

Like all good things, the concept of collaborative divorce developed a life of its own. Straying from its simple initial focus, it has tried to accomplish too much. This type of divorce takes a team of experts approach, making various professionals available, including the attorney, to handle any disputes that arise. Depending on the needs of each divorcing couple, marriage counselors, financial planners specializing in division of assets, mediators, realtors and mortgage brokers, even employment specialists are provided, each charging a separate fee, all agreeing to provide their services in accord with the rules developed by the "collaborative method of divorce."

The goals are certainly admirable: trying to help the couple understand what the other party wants; making the experience less confrontational; focusing on what is best for the family members as a whole, short of reconciliation; and helping them get through the divorce process with improved communication skills that will allow for peaceful interaction between them. The main problem with this, however, is that every member of the team is first committed to the goal of the collaborative divorce movement, not to the individual clients they are hired to represent.

You can only get a collaborative divorce if you use a collaborative attorney dedicated to the cause. If you want, or need, to go to court, the committed attorney will send you elsewhere. Couples sent for mandatory marriage counseling will find that the counselors on the team are really divorce coaches. They are not there to work with the couple to see if the marriage is salvageable. They are there to coach them on how to proceed smoothly through the divorce process.

Today, reconstructive marriage counseling is virtually a thing of the past. My son told me how difficult the counseling session was. There was not one minute spent on the problems of the marriage or why the divorce process had begun, only on how to divorce with the least negative effect on the couple's children.

I began to refer to collaborative divorce as "the warm and fuzzy female divorce." Women, especially the ones who are initiating the divorce and have feelings of guilt for breaking up the marriage, are definitely attracted to this kind of divorce process. They may push collaborative divorce by citing the reasonable cost and speed, reasons that might prove very attractive to a shell-shocked husband. For the wife, the real attraction may be that it appears less threatening and confrontational. It also might be appealing to couples without children who have very few assets to divide.

WARNING: most attorneys specializing in collaborative divorce law keep emphasizing the fact that these divorces are kept out of court. This also means that the attorney specializing in this kind of law may not have much court experience. Court proceedings, however, on behalf of children under the age of majority may be required well past the granting of the divorce decree. There can be problems or adjustments in custody, schooling, child support and/or alimony, travel expenses, and out of state residency. If a collaborative divorce is preferred, it might be advisable to seek out an attorney with both collaborative divorce law experience and court litigation experience. This can be the best of both options.

As a result of the needs developed from this new approach to divorce, a billion-dollar divorce industry was born. Suddenly aware of all the economic opportunities being created, professionals of all types lost no time jumping on the bandwagon to provide the services that were needed. Related businesses, following the parade, developed all the various products that could make the divorce process easier, before and afterward. Software was developed to create shared parenting plans and the visitation calendars needed to go with them. DVDs, audiotapes and books on the strategies and little known tactics of family law are all available on the Internet or at your local bookstores.

Why, the divorced even have their own magazines! A good one, by the way, is called, naturally, *Divorce Magazine*. It is a good place to find out about all the products available. Products have been developed such as cell phones for children with the pre-programmed phone numbers of each parent, and best of all, web cams and Skype that should be mandated by all divorce agreements. These allow children and their non-custodial parent to share real visual quality time, several times a week.

You can even purchase forms and books to help you get your own divorce without an attorney, something not recommended if there are children involved. Parenting plan examples, showing the allocation of parental responsibilities and decision-making, are also available to download on the Internet. There is even a web site on helping someone make a decision as to whether to get a divorce or not. There is also an article for a bitter and frustrated father entitled, "How to Not Get Screwed in a Dirty Divorce, Child Support, Custody or Family Law Fight," by Anthony Comparetto. No example of a collaborative divorce there.

Father's Rights

A father's rights movement developed as more fathers began to understand what a loss they had suffered by being separated from their children. Father's rights advocates continue to fight for family law to be modified in all states. One modification should be a rebuttable presumption of joint custody in all divorces. They are making increased inroads every year as more fathers than ever are being granted custody.

With all these changes to marriage and divorce, grandparents will no longer be able to expect families of today to look and act like families did in their day. The "Honey, I'm home" family has almost ceased to exist. The traditional nuclear family is no longer the structure in which the majority of American children are being raised.

In 2010 the Pew Research Center identified the new economic trend of working wives and mothers as "The Rise of Wives." Co-authors Richard Frey and D'Vera Cohn found that in one out of five marriages, women are more educated and earn more money than their husbands. The main finding of this report was that a gender role reversal appeared to be occurring that resulted for the first time in marriage becoming very economically beneficial for the husband. But this very "Rise of the Wives" resulting from women's increase in economic independence has also given women who are unhappy in their marriages their newly gained option of divorce.

Mix-Master Family

Some divorced women and men, however, choose to give marriage another try. When two households are joined by remarriage, the term applied is "binuclear family." It is estimated that one-third of all children will be living in a stepfamily at some point in their lives, which will make the predominant family in the twenty-first century the binuclear family. These families are made up of semi-related people, some unmarried and some remarried. The adult male figure is the stepfather. This means that in many cases the stepfather's children are being raised in some other single-parent home or binuclear family with someone else's father. Clear lines of authority in the home can definitely get confused.

In many of the two family mix-master households, the parents treat their own children differently than their stepchildren. This happens whether they intend to or not. An interesting exercise is to call up and listen to the voice message on the phone of a mix-master family and see if the parent leaving the message doesn't list his or her children first, ahead of their "steps," regardless of age. The stability of remarriage is definitely threatened by any conflict between stepparent and "steps" (stepchildren). Seventeen percent of remarriages which include "steps" for both husband and wife break up within three years.

Your grandchildren might sometimes be forced to deal with not only one divorce, but multiple divorces. Changes in homes and unrelated housemates often leave them feeling insecure and frustrated. With repeat offenders, when there are more than two house-holds involved, the term usually applied is step/blended families, or "patchwork." This author refers to them as mix-master families.

Once I was more aware of the major changes to marriage and divorce that had occurred since "my day," I felt, maybe a little old, but at least not out of it. Being prepared, I felt I could now contribute effectively in helping my family survive the impending divorce. I hope you do too. Ready or not, it is time to embrace a new day: our children and grandchildren's day.

Rule Two:
Your Day Is Done

Rule Three

Do No Harm

As I collected all the information I felt I needed to help my son with his divorce, I started to think about sharing it with other grandparents who must be looking for help with their own family situations. At first I felt that I was being presumptuous; after all, there was no Ph.D. after my name. Then I realized that what I had been seeking when I first heard about divorce in my family was someone to share his or her experience with me, a grandmother or grandfather who understood and could give me a heads-up on what living with the divorce really means.

Granted, I am not a professional, but how many grandparents are? I am a grandmother, unexpectedly finding myself placed in an unwanted situation. It is my hope that by sharing my experiences and preparations for the anticipated challenges, I will be able to relate enough experiences to be of help to other grandparents who are just starting their journey through the rough divorce terrain. So with no Ph.D., but helpful information learned in the front lines, I'd like to share it all with you.

In the beginning of "THE DIVORCE," I kept thinking, "I didn't even see it coming," but that was not completely honest. It was more that I refused to accept the signs that were there. The sudden lack of calls from my daughter-in-law should have been my first clue. The growing length of time since their last visit should have been another. I was unwilling to view them in a negative light, never considering that they were signs of a marriage breaking down. It is so easy to give excuses for a busy young family.

When the "D" word happens in your family, don't beat yourself up. Facing reality can be scary, but you can't hide from the truth any longer. Facing the fact that your child is about to go through a divorce will not be easy. Turn to your spouse, if you have one, or even an ex-spouse, your child's other parent. Your child will definitely need support from both of you. If you have no living spouse, current or former, seek out another relative or friend, one not connected to the divorce, as your sounding board. Choose your confidant wisely, someone you can trust to keep your feelings about the divorce to himself or herself.

This is not the time to place additional burdens on your child or grandchildren. It is completely unrealistic to expect them to be able to deal with your emotional needs at the same time they are dealing with their own. If necessary, turn to your clergyman or a counselor to help you, but don't be surprised if you get the "It's not about you" response. After all, grandparents are the unacknowledged victims of divorce.

In the beginning I found myself mourning the family life as it had been. But I found it helped to turn my attention to planning on how to contribute positively to the new family structure. I had to keep reminding myself that whatever I did in the future, the past should always remain part of the family. It's like an elephant in the room; you can't forget it, you can't ignore it. But you can forge a careful trail around it.

My grandchildren would have to be shown that the good times we had shared together as a family would be remembered, not just by them, but by everyone in the family. As their grandmother, I would have to keep thinking of ways to reinforce their fragile memories, since they were only two and a half and four when the divorce began. I wanted to make sure they didn't get the impression that any of us regretted their parents' marriage, especially since it had produced such precious children.

In the beginning stages of the separation and divorce, I found it helpful to take a step back and keep myself emotionally in control as much as possible. Being three thousand miles away made it easier for me to stay out of the way and keep silent, but even for a grandparent who is close by, it would be helpful to keep a distance. I felt that keeping separated from all of the emotional garbage my child and grandchildren were being forced to deal with on a daily basis would help me avoid slipping on any hidden banana peels.

That was an important consideration to me, because the last time I had been with my family, I had fallen during a shopping excursion with my grandsons and daughter-in-law, breaking both of my ankles. I guess being taken shopping in the middle of Hurricane Ivan should have been an added clue to some of the other disturbing things I noticed around me. The surgery that followed and being in a wheelchair for three months helped to focus my attention away from any of my worries about my son's marriage.

Once the divorce in the family was announced, my concern, just like yours will be, was on the family situation. My first inclination was to lash out, demanding answers to all those unasked questions, but thank goodness I avoided the temptation. Grandparents, you see, don't have the right to demand anything. And you can create additional problems if you try to interfere in a family crisis you probably don't thoroughly understand yet.

It's hard for grandfathers and grandmothers to accept that consideration of their feelings about the divorce has a very low position on the divorce totem pole. It is very natural to place us on the bottom of the pole like the older generations who preceded us, in a position appropriately symbolizing the weight-bearing task we will carry for the generations that follow. At no time will the weight of the family's problems seem as heavy as when there is an imminent divorce in the family. Even though we have no part in the original decision to divorce, we are nevertheless deeply affected by it. We are in a position to give much-needed support to everyone else in the family, as long as we do so without inflicting any additional damage to an already volatile situation. "DO NO HARM" must be the mantra of the day.

I kept reminding myself I was merely sitting on the sidelines on this one. I was supporting the team, like I had when my sons played Pop Warner football. Before I was ready to speak out, I carefully weighed the pros and cons of the opinions and advice I was on the verge of expressing. I kept hoping that when I did speak up, whatever I said would not sound like I was preaching.

My first attempt failed miserably. I could see my son rolling his eyes even over the phone wires. I knew I would have to go back to thinking out what I should say, remembering that how I planned to express myself was as important as what I was going to say. Everyone hates to hear "I told you so," especially when they are vulnerable and failed to heed prior warnings. So even if I was filled with negative thoughts about his soon-to-be ex, I had to repress them.

Facilitator, Please!

One of the hardest parts of parenting and grandparenting is reaching the right level of parental involvement, deciding when your intervention is appropriate, appreciated and not intrusive. You don't want to be thought of as indifferent, but on the other hand, you don't want to be perceived as butting in where you are not wanted.

Grandparents have such different views on parenting. Grandmothers feel they are a success if their children and grandchildren still need them, while grandfathers feel successful if their children don't. In keeping with this different perspective, a grandmother's first instinct is to try and rescue her child from unpleasant problems that are taking an emotional toll. I guess it reminds her of when her child was small and ran to her to kiss his boo-boos away. A grandfather's first instinct is to sit down with his child to discuss the practical side of the divorce, questioning the couple's financial situation, the plans his child has made for the immediate future, and what help he can offer to carry them out. Whatever your instinct, hold back until your child has a chance to consider the pros and cons for himself or herself.

The greatest help I can offer in this book is to suggest that you always treat your child, son or daughter, as the adult he or she has become. Respect your child's ability to handle his or her role as a parent responsibly. Both grandmothers and grandfathers need to think of themselves as facilitators, not rescuers. It will never be an intrusion if you share with your child that you have total faith in his or her decisions and you intend to do anything you can to help your child implement them. I know that there will be times you might not feel your child is handling things as you would. But that is the perfect time to keep a sensitive step back to show that you are there to assist in what has to be done, but not to make the decisions for him or her.

At first some grandparents may find it impossible to approve their child's decision to divorce, confused and fearful as they are by what uncertainty lies ahead. Accepting your child's decision to divorce doesn't have to mean you agree with it, or even approve. It can just be a kind of acknowledgement, like the Japanese expression "hai," which instead of always meaning "yes," can also mean, "I acknowledge you are speaking to me," but not necessarily "I understand or agree with what you are saying."

Respecting your child's right to find solutions for his or her own problems, even if mistakes are made along the way, will help him or her build up much-needed self-esteem. The more your child deals with on his or her own, the more prepared he or she will be to handle what is ahead. Showing that you accept your child's opinions and decisions might prove to create the perfect climate to enable you to form a new, deeper adult relationship, one that might never have existed between you before.

Don't worry, your opportunity to help out will present itself. Just be patient. The volume of problems created by the divorce can be so overwhelming that even the most accomplished of our children are going to look to their parents for guidance, or even just a sounding board. But first they have to gain control of that defensive response which automatically develops with the plans for the divorce. At this point grandparents will be in a position to either give positive reinforcement, or to do a great deal of harm, so be very careful when offering your opinions or advice. If you are married grandparents, make sure both of you present a united front when offering advice. Conflicting opinions will just complicate things. Be understanding if your child doesn't follow all your advice, but be assured your suggestions will not have fallen on deaf ears.

I knew my son was reaching out to me when he came to visit me just a few weeks after he had dropped the D bomb. I didn't have to imagine how vulnerable he was, because the first thing he required was a trip to the doctor, who diagnosed him with pneumonia. His illness, it seemed, was a blessing in disguise, because his recovery provided just the time we both needed to discuss what was ahead for him.

I was so tempted at first to become a "Divorce Assassin," spewing a poisonous diatribe of harmful personal attacks against my in-law child, but I resisted. Being emotionally involved made it very tempting to lose all control of my tongue. I realized my son was too sick for that. What he needed first was some tea and sympathy, and he was in the best place for that at home. Of course, the antibiotics were doing their job too.

At first, while sitting at the kitchen table over lunch, tea in hand, I tried a little of the Rudelson humor our family was famous for. We always use humor to deflect that little black "Joe Btfsplk rain cloud" whenever it hovers over us. But I quickly realized my son wasn't ready to see anything amusing in his divorce situation. I kept working on keeping my sense of humor in check and under control by recognizing it for what it was, a sort of nervous tic that I had developed a long time ago to deal with all the painful situations in my life.

And the thought came to me that, in comporting myself to help my son, I too was now changing and growing. I was so grateful my son was home with me while he was recuperating. It proved to me that focusing on helping him and my grandchildren was definitely the way to survive this divorce in our family.

One Mouth, Two Ears

Once my son was feeling stronger, something told me I could be of the greatest help by simply listening. This was one of those times since my husband's death that his absence was being felt more strongly than ever by both of us. The responsibility of being the only parent had never felt as heavy on my shoulders as it did at that moment.

Sometimes when he was awake, I would go into his bedroom/my office and sit at my computer to answer my e-mail. But in truth, it was to make myself available to listen to anything he wanted to get off his chest. As I listened to what he had to say, I kept thinking that the reason I was born with only one mouth but two ears was so I could listen twice as much as I talked. It gave me time to filter my thoughts between my mind and my mouth, helping me to control that nagging temptation to play devil's advocate.

I found that actually listening to what he was saying proved to be the best way to educate myself about what was going on. It gave me the chance to concentrate, one hundred percent, on what was being said, instead of thinking about what I was going to say next. I not only heard the words spoken, but all the emotion behind them. He did a lot of venting in the beginning, but because I understand people do that most to the ones they love, I did my best not to take it personally. But I have to be honest, I did get frightened and upset by the amount of rage and anger he spewed forth, even though I knew he was just expressing all the hurt and betrayal he was feeling.

It wasn't easy to keep myself from being consumed by my son's feelings. I kept reminding myself, over and over, *this is not about you*, but I was left weakened and depressed anyway. I was so frustrated and angry that I was left with an overwhelming urge to be drawn into the fray, but I knew that would only make everything that much harder. While I continued to listen, I had to work hard on remaining objective and impartial. I'll admit it was so painful to hear how much he was suffering. I forced myself to stay seated at my desk, all the time fighting the temptation to flee.

I knew he was grateful to have been given the chance to express his feelings to someone who loved him unconditionally, who wouldn't criticize him for the way he was feeling. During that conversation he was not looking for advice from me; he just needed my affirmation that he was thinking clearly and that he was headed in the right direction, something I gladly gave.

When you have those first discussions with your child, your active listening will demonstrate the respect you have for your child, something which will surely be appreciated. At this early stage it is best if you don't express how you are feeling. Your child is not really ready to hear it.

Keep listening to your child's complaints, but listen quietly. Whatever you do, avoid "Parent Interruptus." That is a real conversation killer. Periods of silence are not a bad thing. They don't need to be filled at the first opportunity, especially by those insipid comments. You know, the ones that point out that there might be a positive side to divorce, like "It might be for the best," "A chance to make a new start," or "All those fish in the sea," etc. Anyone going through this divorce nightmare is in no shape to hear those insensitive bromides from people who do not know what to say, yet pass them out like aspirin.

We were sitting at the end of dinner one night, several days after my son had arrived, when I finally felt the time had come to express myself, that he was finally strong enough physically to hear me. The first thing I did was to assure my son I would always be there to assist him in any way I could. As his mother, I told him, my main goal was always going to be to help him nurture and strengthen his relationship with his children, my grandchildren.

Some of you may have the opportunity to listen to your in-law child's side too, but proceed with caution. Try to listen to your child first so you can have a complete picture of the situation. I was never given the opportunity to hear what my soon to be ex-daughter-in-law had to say. But I was warned by some of my friends that such a conversation would probably end badly. I would proceed at my own peril. My friends advised me to give my child's spouse the right to express her feelings, as long as she could do so without becoming abusive, either to me or about my child. It was suggested that if the other parent keeps trying to get you to side with him or her, don't argue the point, just acknowledge that you love your grandchildren and your goal is to always be there for them. The choice to listen or not is mine, they told me. But if the conversation became a dumping ground, I was to head out the door, or if on the phone or texting, immediately end the communication attempt for that day.

Helping Hand

After I felt I had been brought up to date on the decisions that my son had already made, I was ready to give more active support on the decisions that would have to be made in the near future. I avoided making suggestions unless they were warranted, but admittedly I overstepped my boundaries several times.

What proved to be the most helpful was that by the time my son had arrived home, I was prepared to discuss his divorce with him. The few weeks prior to my son's arrival had given me the chance to do some research on what decisions my son was going to be required to make in the immediate future. That preparation proved to be worth every minute of the effort.

During that first week my son slowly began to regain his strength, until he was finally able to focus on how much had to be accomplished in the weeks and months ahead. I shared with him some of the information I had entered into my computer as well as some of the books on divorce I had been using for my research.

When we got to the subject of his need for new living arrangements, I offered my help in furnishing a new bedroom for my grandsons. I showed him some of the catalogues I had put aside that would allow me, even from three thousand miles away, to be able to put it all together. All choices, I told him, would be with his approval. We could do it all on the computer.

It was then I introduced him to the concept of "Mommy's House and Daddy's House." It was the first time I saw my son smile since he had arrived. The thought that he would be able to provide a real home for his sons when they were with him gave him his first glimpse into what life could be as a real family after the separation and the divorce had been granted. He realized he could be a real presence in their lives, not just a visitor. It was his first look into a picture of divorce, not as one of loss for him, but as gaining a chance to be a 24/7 dad, even if it was not going to be 365 days of the year. He finally had a clear goal of what he would insist on in the divorce. First he knew he would have to find out where Daddy's House was going to be. As a college professor, he had decided to relocate as a good way to start his new life.

After my son recognized his two top priorities, a job search and research into what his rights were in the divorce, he started to work to achieve them. As soon as he was feeling well enough, we made a trip down to our local bookstore. When we left the store, he was loaded down with books on divorce for him and several books on divorce for his sons. We celebrated his first day out and about by going to lunch at one of our favorite restaurants. We spread the books out on the table in front of us. Both of us couldn't help smiling at the adorable, upbeat illustrations in the ones he had bought for his sons. For some reason, buying books called *Dinosaurs Divorce*, *It's Not Your Fault*, *KoKo-Bear* and *Mommy's House and Daddy's House* made him feel he was better prepared to break the news about the divorce to his sons.

Acquiring those books seemed to empower him, and he suddenly had the energy to start moving forward. It was a pleasure watching him sit at his computer busying himself making lists. In order to make a start on the new home he intended to make for himself and his sons, he made a list of the things he needed to take with him from his marital home. I must admit I made a few suggestions to add to the list that would help me furnish my grandchildren's bedroom with things that were familiar to them. The next was a list of the documents he needed to gather in order to start the divorce procedure. My son and I have always had an extremely close relationship, but working together on something this important definitely brought us even closer. Hopefully he understood he wouldn't have to go through this alone.

There are many things that any grandparent can do to help his or her divorcing child. If you live close enough, you might be able to help with house hunting, provide babysitting time to allow your child, or even your in-law, to go on job interviews, or in some cases temporarily help with financial arrangements until the divorce is completed. Some grandparents even offer to share housing and become built-in babysitters. Of course, when any moving occurs, a grandfather's strong arms, and maybe even a truck, would really come in handy. Grandmothers are great at packing up kitchens. I don't know why; it must be in their genes.

Attorney Search

One of the most important decisions your child is going to have to make, after the word "divorce" raises its ugly head, is selecting an attorney to do the legal work to actually obtain the divorce. The selection can be a daunting task at first, with many suggestions coming from every direction. It seems that everyone has a first or second cousin practicing law.

To make it even more stressful for your child, you might find that some of his or her friends are singing the praises of the new in thing in ending a marriage, collaborative divorce. To a vulnerable spouse, the explanation that this kind of divorce will prove more economical and a less stressful way to go may make it sound attractive. But the pressure to obtain a new type of divorce that the husband or wife is not familiar with might make the choice even more confusing.

This was one of the things my son wanted to talk over with me while he was home. He wanted to find out what a collaborative divorce really entailed and whether choosing this kind of divorce made sense for him. He didn't want to make such an important decision without understanding it. Certainly I was not a lawyer, but because I had met his father in law school and had ended up managing two very large law firms after I had been widowed, he knew I could get the answers for him.

My son wasn't a stranger to the law. One of his first playrooms was his father's law office. His father would take him with him for an early court appearance before dropping him off at nursery school, and he was a witness in the trial regarding his father's death when he was only fifteen. During high school he had worked after school in the law office I managed, and when he was only nineteen he worked in Hong Kong for the largest law firm in the world. I was confident in his ability to prepare himself for what was necessary.

The first thing I encouraged my son to do was to become familiar with the language of divorce and then to do some research on what his rights were, especially concerning types of custody. "Don't allow anyone to make you feel guilty for taking time to determine what your rights are or to insist on those rights," I told him.

Collaborative divorce was something both my son and I wanted to understand more about. Because it is the more attractive cost option, it appears to have become the "divorce du jour." But collaborative divorce, we discovered, should be selected only after careful thought and education. The proponents of this kind of divorce promote it as a more positive and cooperative manner of divorce and a less confrontational way of handling disagreements. But, as with anything that looks too attractive, there are problems, one of which can end up being costly. In a collaborative divorce, the couple and their attorneys must sign an agreement that they will not go to court.

The problem arises if there is a contested motion or issue that requires court action. Then the lawyer practicing collaborative divorce exclusively must withdraw from representation, and the couple has to start the attorney search all over again. That can in the end turn a less expensive divorce into a more costly one. There is a solution, however; some trial attorneys have qualified also as collaborative divorce attorneys. The challenge then becomes to select the best lawyer who will be there to "watch your child's back."

I was adamant about doing a proper search for an attorney because a few years before, I had done such a poor job selecting a personal injury attorney for myself. Without checking, I had selected an attorney a friend had recommended. You can imagine my dismay when I found out that someone had issued a "hit" on my new attorney's life. Oh, that isn't the worst of the story. When the case was ready to go to trial, the attorney had simply disappeared, never to be seen again. By the time I got wind of it after my chemo treatments, my case had been dismissed. It took a lot of legal expertise by a new lawyer to get the court to allow the case to be reopened.

You might think that a grandmother or grandfather can't possibly be of help to his or her child as he makes this critical selection, but the exact opposite is true. A grandparent is in the perfect position to help his or her child gather a list of attorneys to interview. For example, you probably have a much wider source of referrals available to you, not connected in any way to your child's spouse. You may also have more time available to conduct a more thorough inquiry.

Reaching out to your relatives, friends and business associates might yield some good recommendations of competent family law attorneys. For a daughter, you might want to look for one who represents women. For a son, find a father's rights specialist. If you know anyone whose child is recently divorced, ask him or her which attorney was used, and most importantly, if his or her family was satisfied with the results. Also find out if the parties elected to have a collaborative divorce, and would they recommend it for your son or daughter?

If your early search for an attorney doesn't produce any good results, check with the professionals in your life, or the State Bar of the state where the attorney is needed. By the way, don't forget, like I did, to check with the State Bar to see if there have been any disciplinary actions taken against the attorney your child is thinking of retaining. If all else fails, you might even find a great attorney by using the Internet, especially if your grandchildren have been moved to a new legal jurisdiction you are not familiar with.

Before finalizing the list, identify which of the lawyers are qualified as family law trial attorneys as well as collaborative divorce attorneys, and include the names and phone numbers of the people who have made the recommendations for each attorney. Once your child is armed with the list of recommended attorneys, he or she is prepared to start interviewing them. So that the interview process does not prove too overwhelming, suggest that after your child makes a determination of the most promising lawyers on the list, he or she then set up interviews with the top three choices first. Your child may be lucky and find the perfect choice among those first three.

While my son was still with me at home, he asked me to start the search. I lived on the other side of the country from where he needed representation, but I still knew I could help. I immediately went into my bedroom, spread pad and phone book out in front of me on my bed, and started making calls. I started first with relatives who lived in or near the state where my son was residing. Little by little the list began to grow.

The whole search had lasted just a few hours when I finally hit the jackpot. The process could have been a little faster, but each call had to include time for my relatives to commiserate about the imminent divorce. To be polite, I also had to listen to a litany of all the other problems in their respective families, including recent news about other relatives' divorces, but that of course was why I had called. I needed information.

At last I knew I had found the information I needed. My cousin, it turned out, had a cousin, not related to me, who was a judge in a neighboring state just ten miles from my son. I was pretty sure he would be able to recommend the perfect person as well as answer our concerns about collaborative divorce attorneys. As I hurried into my son's room with the good news and phone number, I felt the first sense of relief since I had heard about the divorce. I just knew that my son would be in good hands.

My son left for home with an appointment to meet with the judge the next day. When he was directed by the judge to a former associate who practiced in the state my son lived in, the attorney search was almost over. The interview with that attorney revealed that he was not only a family law trial attorney, but a collaborative divorce attorney as well. The best of both worlds. Problem solved. Search over. I guess those cousins who practice law sometimes can prove very helpful after all. Who knew?

Tips for Choosing an Attorney

Your child might not find an attorney as easily as my son did, but that is no reason to be discouraged. The selection of your child's divorce attorney is almost like selecting a new best friend his or her first day at summer camp, only with better preparation. Close attention to details is going to have a big influence on this selection, because your child will want to select someone who will make him or her feel comfortable. After all, your child is going to have to spend a great deal of stressful time with the attorney.

Even if your child has had a lot of prior experience dealing with or being represented by attorneys, encourage him or her to be very prepared for that first interview. Bringing copies of the marriage license, names and current addresses of the parties to the divorce, social security numbers, information concerning any prior divorce, if any, and copies of birth certificates of all children born of the current union might help move the meeting along. It also might be helpful to bring a written statement of what has led up to seeking the divorce. Financial documentation is usually provided once the attorney is selected, but it might be a good idea to gather it all together to be prepared.

Considering the following questions might help your child in selecting an attorney after the first interview:

1. Were you invited in right away when you arrived for your meeting? If not, were you treated in such a manner that you felt your time was being respected?

2. Did the attorney ask the secretary to hold all calls, so your meeting would not be interrupted?

3. Did the attorney explain where he or she is licensed to practice, and whether he or she can go to court to represent you if necessary? If the attorney only practices collaborative divorce, did he or she explain the benefits and limitations to that type of divorce to your satisfaction?

4. Did the attorney clearly, without appearing condescending, explain what steps the divorce process will take? Advancements in women's rights or not, how an attorney treats a female client is something to pay close attention to.

5. Was anything discussed about protecting the family assets from being squandered, removed or hidden? Were you given any insight about how to go about marshaling the family assets for valuation? Or how child support, alimony or asset distribution will be determined?

6. Did you feel all the legal rights of a divorcing spouse were explained thoroughly, and were all your questions answered to your satisfaction?

7. Did the attorney explain what custody options were available to you, how they differ from each other, and which choice the

attorney would recommend in your case, or which type the attorney thinks you could obtain easily and which with difficulty?

8. Were you given a chance to explain the issues leading to your decision to divorce; your wishes in terms of child custody, child support, alimony or settlement; and what specific problems you anticipate occurring during the divorce process? Was the attorney ever acquainted with your spouse? Did you feel the attorney listened to what you had to say, or did all the talking instead?

9. Did the attorney indicate how long he or she thought it would take to obtain the final divorce decree and explain what type of services would be available from his or her office after the divorce decree is obtained? Will he or she be able to handle any changes to child support, alimony, or the custody agreement in the future? Lastly, did the attorney discuss what changes might be necessary when an ex-spouse goes to work, remarries, loses a job, relocates the children to another jurisdiction, suffers financial reverses, or becomes ill or dies?

10. Was the cost for the divorce explained, and did the fees seem fair and equitable?

11. Did you feel the attorney would protect your rights, guide you to make the best decisions for you and your children, and support those decisions during all stages of the divorce process and after? Did you feel that the attorney seemed genuinely concerned about you and the outcome of your divorce? Did you feel the attorney was someone whom you and others could communicate with easily?

12. If the attorney is practicing in a law firm, were you assured that you could depend on that attorney, not someone else in his or her firm, to handle your divorce personally at all stages of the process, including representing you at any hearings in court? And will that attorney be willing to include that in any retainer agreement? Believe it or not, this can become a problem if after you are signed up with one attorney, another attorney you have never met takes over at a critical time. And lastly, be sure to indicate that you

expect any confidences with the attorney to be kept under attorney-client privilege, including the initial interview.

Once the interviews are completed, picking the best lawyer doesn't have to be complicated. It can be as simple as choosing the one who makes you feel at ease, was neither judgmental nor condescending, and who can be trusted to keep his or her client's best interest in focus in every action the attorney takes.

Of course, you could select an attorney the way one of my friends did. She told me a good friend had referred her to her divorce lawyer. When she called him for an appointment, she explained she needed to get a divorce, but before she scheduled an appointment with him, she needed to know how big he was. The attorney assured her he was physically a very big man, if that was what she meant. In fact, he said, he was a retired Marine.

Satisfied by the attorney's response, she went ahead and scheduled the appointment. Intrigued, the attorney asked her why his size was so important to her. She answered, "Because my husband has a gun and threatened to kill me, our children and anyone I hire to represent me. I needed to know if you could physically take care of yourself and hopefully take care of me and my children as well." He must have done a great job, because after the divorce was granted, she married him. Yes, they lived happily ever after.

Sadly, her ex-husband did use his gun, but thankfully, instead of turning it on his family, he used it on himself. It is hard to contemplate, but divorce can in some cases turn out to be a life-and-death matter, and in all situations it should be taken very seriously.

Even though there may now be no-fault divorce in every state, for the first meeting after the selection of attorney is made, it might be helpful to bring a chronological description of the events leading up to the decision to divorce. This way the attorney can get a clear picture of the situation and the other party he or she will be required to deal with. If there have been any abusive behavior issues, a list of the dates, photos, if any, and details of each incidence should be brought to the attention of the attorney.

Facing It

Once the attorney is retained, his or her advice given and the divorce underway, the best way for the grandparents to help their child move forward is to step back. For the moment, keep yourself out of the way, waiting for a specific request for assistance. It might be frustrating, but keeping out of the way will produce the most helpful results.

Before they will know how you can be of help, your daughters and sons need to face what the reality of divorce really means. The first and hardest part of the separation of husband and wife comes immediately once the divorce process has begun. The couple divides into two separate addresses, each home requiring financial support. The money which once paid for one home now must pay for two. "Mommy's House and Daddy's House" comes with a high price tag, and it will require a great deal of adjustment and sacrifice to make ends meet.

For the husband and father with the stay-at-home wife, this will probably be one of the most insecure moments of his life as he realizes all the extra expenses and responsibilities he will be required to meet. For the wife, it is a time of terror when she has to come to grips with the fact she must get a job but hasn't worked since her I Do's. She also has no idea yet what kind of support she can expect from her husband. Certainly she doesn't even want to think about what will happen if her husband fails to provide what she needs. Unsure about what kind of employment she will be able to secure, she wonders if her earning potential will enable her to bring in enough to add to the limited support from her soon to be ex-husband.

The working wife has it a little easier. She at least knows what income she can count on. What will become immediately apparent to the newly single mother, however, whether she is working or not, is the loss of the additional pair of hands she has come to depend on in times of crisis. Both husband and wife will miss that shoulder they have come to lean on. When each party calls up his or her bank or credit card company to notify them that he or she is no longer responsible for the debt of the other, the full weight of what the term "divorced" really means will start to sink in.

Few wives can count on huge settlements and monthly spousal and child support from the husbands they are divorcing. For most wives the alimony picture may not be too comforting, and the child support she will probably be awarded could be nowhere near what she expected. Especially since now it is based on a specific support schedule.

For some of those newly single mothers who are awarded temporary spousal support for a period long enough to achieve an educational goal, there are now some grants available. The only problem is that in the beginning stages of the divorce, many mothers are in no emotional condition to handle going to class, taking care of home and children, and handling family finances alone too. Grandmothers and grandfathers, you might both be called in to help out with some of this overload, especially if in addition the single mother has to carry the weight of a temporary job.

This is a really hard time for the husband as well. Hopefully he is already employed, but the difficult thing for him is that the financial demands of support payments that have to be paid each month seem to shrink the salary amount he has been used to.

One of the worst possible scenarios for a single mother is having an ex-husband who gets so overwhelmed by the increased responsibilities that he simply disappears. When this happens, and in some unfortunate divorces it does, the ex-husband not only disappears, but leaves a huge debt behind which the ex-wife is legally responsible for. Some husbands are so determined to escape from spousal and/or child support, they actually leave the country, and then it is almost impossible to reach them legally.

An older woman I worked with had been awarded lifetime spousal support after a long marriage. Her husband was so determined not to pay her that he left the country with a new wife. The biggest problem was that her daughter, an adult child of divorce, so blamed her mother for her parents' divorce that she wouldn't give her mother her father's address.

Several years later, after the wife had unsuccessfully tried every legal way to get all the back support payments due her, she heard her vindictive ex was returning to the states for their daughter's wedding. She was faced with a King Solomon-like decision: a process server waiting at the church, or letting her daughter's father walk her down the aisle? Her daughter would never speak to her again if she chose the first, or, if she allowed her ex to escape his court-ordered spousal support yet again, she would need to work for the rest of her life. She made the only decision a loving mother could make. She is still working.

Father's Crusade

One of the hardest times in the whole divorce was the day my son had to say goodbye to his sons as they were moved out of the family home. I stayed by the phone all day worrying about how he would take such a devastating experience.

It was too early in the divorce process for my son to appreciate that a great change had occurred with the modern-day divorce that was going to positively affect his life with his sons. More recently the courts and child psychologists have recognized the need children of divorce have for more equal time spent with both parents. It is now understood that permanent harm has been inflicted on children in divorced homes by limiting the time of one parent in favor of the other. This change has, for the first time, questioned the myth—which had raised motherhood to sainthood status— that mothers are the only parent able to provide the nurturing their children require.

All my son understood, when he kissed and hugged his sons, ages two and a half and four, goodbye, trying to keep the tears back until they drove away, was that they were leaving with their mother. As in most divorces, she had been given residential custody. It didn't make him feel any better to know that forty percent of American children live without their father in their home. All he knew was that his children were being deprived of having their father with them, the loss of which my son, having lost his father at the age of ten, understood better than anyone.

After the moving van left with the remnants of his family's belongings, he went to the phone and called me. He sounded so emotionally exhausted as he described the last few hours before the children left. I tried to reassure him that nothing would interfere with his role as their father, but three thousand miles away, I felt helpless as the words left my lips. Nobody had to tell him that a father is an important role model to his children. My son knew that firsthand. He said that the day his boys were taken away from his home and the day his father died would always be the worst days of his life.

He shared his biggest fear with me. Did I think the boys would sustain the same kind of emotional damage he had, the result of the absence of their father's loving influence in their lives on a daily basis? I reminded him that his children still had him. Oh, he said he was thankful for that, but he realized that due to the limited amount of time he was going to get to spend with them as the non-residential parent, it was going to take a crusade, or at the very least, a great deal of extra effort and creativity on his part, to make sure that the damage would be mitigated and that his relationship with his sons would be insured. I told him that I knew he would find a way.

Then to sort of change the subject, I asked him what it was like in the house after they left, and how many days he had to wait there alone before he moved out too. He told me the house was so empty with almost all of the furniture gone. There were boxes and some furniture left for him to move in three days to his new apartment in a new state, for his new job. He assured me there was a bed left for him, a couch, some chairs, his desk, a beautiful cabinet that his wife had restored, and of course, the chest of drawers he had moved to every house he had ever lived in since he graduated, the one he had had since the day he was born. He had the beautiful pieces of Chinese porcelain I had given them and the some of the artwork purchased during their marriage. And of course, of the wood carved skeleton bride and groom they had brought back from their time in Mexico, there was only the groom. At least it made me smile when he told me that he also had the coffee table that my grandsons used to play on, making a highway for their little cars, trucks and trains. It was the first piece of furniture they each pulled themselves up to when they first learned to stand.

For the room the boys were going to share, he had the chest of drawers their mother had painted with the Cat in the Hat and other illustrations from Dr. Seuss. It was just perfect for their new home at the college Dr. Seuss's author had attended. I had delivered as promised. My grandsons' new bunk beds were in the boxes they had arrived in, ready to assemble. Also a new dinosaur rug, little dinosaur stools, sheets and comforters to match were boxed and ready. And Raj, the three-foot, black-and-white stuffed tiger that my best friend had given them when they were little, would be my grandsons' familiar friend to guard them when they slept. Everything was ready and waiting to make Daddy's House a home. Even though I felt I had been a help to my son, when I said goodbye and hung up the phone, I wept.

If you have any question about how hard it is for a child who has been raised with a parent—mother or father—absent from the home, just ask a few. They will tell you the toll it takes on them emotionally. Don't bother asking the parent they live with most of the time; he or she won't be able to face the reality of the damage the divorce has inflicted on the children until the parent is forced to recognize the problems his or her children are dealing with as adult children of divorce.

At least my son was grateful that, because it was now recognized that mothers and fathers are expected to share equal responsibility for making the major decisions, he would have equal say regarding his sons' education, religious affiliation, medical care, etc. But he was aware this joint custody designation was just an attempt by the courts to disguise the inequity of the non-custodial parent having so much less time than the other parent. It was a bone thrown to a desperate parent to maintain some kind of control over his own children. In actuality, this does not make up in any way for the inequality, but it is a lot better than in the past, when fathers were just regarded as little better than an ATM machine.

I couldn't help but think how hard it must have been for my grandsons' mother too. She was forced to move to a much smaller place in a new location. I could only imagine how painful it must have been for her, with the help of the maternal grandparents, unpacking all the pieces of her former life with my son. I wondered if she remembered all the happier times, when after their honeymoon they had unpacked in their first home, or moved into the home they had bought with the room for me on the ground floor so I wouldn't have to walk up the stairs.

Were my grandsons crying for their daddy? How was she explaining his absence? We would never know. What memories were produced as each piece was unwrapped, especially the carved wood skeleton bride, each picture hung, and the familiar furniture placed in new positions in Mommy's House?

In most cases it is not the mother and children who leave home first. It is usually the father who moves out, leaving the mother and children to adjust to the sudden empty seat at the family dinner table. A mother usually prefers to stay put in the family home, trying to keep things as much like they were as possible. She is likely to be denying to herself how much things have or will change and trying to convince the children things will remain like they were. One problem they have to deal with, however, is that the family home may be heavily mortgaged, and the monthly payments will place this newly separate family under a severe financial strain.

Wives and mothers who have to leave the family home will find their choices limited. Downsizing, the woman still needs to find an affordable place big enough to house herself and her children and hopefully close to the children's school. To solve the money problem, a single mother does have an option of finding a room-mate, such as another single mother and child, or to move in a grandparent or move herself and her children back to her parents' house. Because the mother is the one most often with residential custody, it is the maternal grandparents that do the most heavy lift-ing.

The only benefit the father might have living by himself is that if his job requires him to work long hours or be on the road most days of the week, he might be free of all those guilt pangs he suffers when he arrives later than expected. Also, maybe he can more easily plan time off for when his children are with him. Regardless of where he finds to live, like the mother, he still is going to have to find an affordable place with enough space to hold him and his children. The worst thing for the father is that when he arrives home, there won't be any little faces smiling at the window and yel-ling "Daddy's home!" when he walks through the door.

The very fact that the mother does not have to suffer the sepa-ration from her children because she is granted residential custody has its own problems. She is the one that will be responsible for handling her children's adjustment to the absence of their father in the home, which includes in many cases her children blaming her for not being able to keep their father from leaving. This occurs regardless which of parent initiated the divorce. What makes this even more difficult is that her children may harbor this resentment for the rest of their lives.

In this kind of atmosphere, she will have to handle all the children's problems alone. The children, with only their mother to act as disciplinarian, plus grant yes or no decisions to their wishes, will resent that they no longer have their father available as arbitrator. And what is the final raw deal for every divorced mother, she will no longer have the best of all parental threats available to keep her kids in line: "Just wait till your father gets home!"

My son's separation from his children was extremely hard on him. Like every divorced father, he missed kissing his sons and hugging them every day when he left for work, having dinner with them, and sometimes bathing them and getting them ready for bed. And most of all, he missed tucking them in and reading them a bedtime story each night before they fell asleep. He only saw them every other weekend, and that weekend only amounted to 48 hours at most, which included an hour and a half of transportation.

But even in that limited time, he found that there was a surprise benefit to the divorce. There was nothing like 24/7 time with his children to develop a greater closeness than he had ever had before. What was amazing to me, a long distance grandmother, was that I found out I had the same benefit when they were with me. But I realized early on that I could do less harm if I kept that surprising benefit my little secret.

Besides dealing with the loss of time with their children, fathers are constantly finding it necessary to deal with the economic repercussions of the divorce. Since no-fault divorce, fathers have been given at least one break, the restructuring of child support, so that now a working mother must also contribute to her children's support. No matter how much equality in divorce is fought for, it will never be enough. The concept of children being divided between two parents and two households can never attain the qualities of equality.

One of the biggest inequities created is when the residential custodian makes the unilateral decision to move far from the other parent due to remarriage or employment. Some do it with the conscious intention of inconveniencing the other parent, preventing him or her from having easy access to the children. In most cases, fighting the move is a no-win situation. For the parent left behind, it is devastating and means a severe increase in expense to see his or her children, and even less time to spend with them.

This truly demands a King Solomon-like response from the parent left behind, who in putting the children's welfare first, has to selflessly disregard his or her own. It is not too surprising that many of the parents left behind, because of the emotional and financial strain, give up the fight.

When it happened to my son, less than a year after his divorce, he knew he would never allow the separation from his children, even one thousand miles away, to destroy his relationship. Suddenly the every other weekend didn't look so bad. He was just going to have to get even more creative in keeping his relationship with his boys as strong as possible.

For me, the long distant grandmother, it just divided my heart into more pieces than before. As soon as they moved so far away from their father, my contact would lessen too. My son wouldn't be the only one that had to get creative; this grandmother would have to get creative too. I was going to have to start making another pitcher of lemonade.

Where Do I Live Today, Mommy?

There will be a lot of adjustments to make for each member of the family once the separation in the family has occurred and the divorce is under way. Each parent is now a separate individual again, living in a separate home. Your grandchildren have homes in two different locations, some as close as across the street, and some as far as thousands of miles away. Grandparents, tread carefully— no matter which location your grandchildren are in, for months, days or hours, be careful of how you refer to it. Try not to think of your grandchildren as weekend guests in your child's home, or in the other parent's home. Your grandchildren are living there, with that parent, not visiting. In this politically correct environment we all find ourselves in, the time a child lives with one parent and then the other is now referred to by some as "parenting time."

Living in two locations is not easy. Give your grandchildren all the support they need, so they don't feel like only temporary visitors in each. My son and I thought that my grandsons would feel more like they were at home if the exchanges between their two homes required no packing, thus no luggage. What it required was special pajamas, underwear and toothbrushes at Daddy's, plus additional clothes and shoes. This is where a grandmother can definitely be useful. I still could select clothes for them, toys and books that are waiting in my grandsons' room for them every time they are at Daddy's House. I am getting really good at Internet shopping. Grandfathers, too, can supply those footballs and soccer balls grandsons need. Oh, of course, for athletic granddaughters too. And what could be better than a large Lego or jigsaw puzzle project that can be worked on when everyone is together?

You might not approve of your grandchildren being moved from one location to another on a regular schedule, but this movement definitely allows your grandchildren to continue to feel close to both parents. As a non-custodial grandparent, I find that it is the only chance I have to keep a close relationship going with my grandchildren. Every time they are with their dad, I can talk to them every day on the phone or visit with them virtually on Skype. Also, at least once a year I come to be with them when they are with their dad. That is such a special time when our whole family can be together.

One thing grandparents need to be very careful of is not to try to explain the divorce or living situation to anyone in front of their grandchildren. The old saying applies, "Little pitchers have big ears." Assume that if they are in the house, they can hear you as if they were in the room. Be sure to choose your words very carefully. Children, especially little ones, are very literal. If they hear you telling someone how sad you are that your grandchildren are now living in a broken home, they can picture their house really broken—or themselves.

As more and more parents remarry, family members are shuffled together in unrelated ways, complicating the relationships within the family structure. The post-divorce family is an entirely new type of family, lacking many of the features of an intact family, and forcing the children who live with their remarried mother to form new types of identities in a family whose members do not even share the same name. This creates the impression to outsiders that it is like a household made up of unrelated individuals, resembling something like a family boarding house.

What's In a Name? Everything!

Very often the children not only have different last names from the other children in the same house, but also have a different name than their own mother. A mother who returns to her maiden name can also have a different name, not only from her children but also from her current husband. You may find that your grandchildren will find it very difficult to adjust to the fact that their mother's name no longer matches theirs. Often they have to deal with being misidentified, continually being required to explain the name difference to their teachers and friends. This is especially hard for young children of divorce, who are just in the process of understanding their identity, learning to spell and write their first and last names.

Children are not the only ones who have problems with their name difference. Mothers have a problem too. There are circumstances that crop up requiring them to prove they are their own children's mother. Picking up a birthday gift at the post office sent to her child, one mother was required to show proof that she lived at the same address before they would turn it over to her. She said she never gets used to it, but it happens all the time.

Fathers also can have problems. A child's father can feel both angry and humiliated if he hears someone addressing his children incorrectly. One afternoon, a father, bringing back his sons to their mother's house, heard one of her friends ask his oldest son how he felt being a middle child. For a moment the child looked up at her in confusion. "I am the oldest child in my family," the boy responded. The new addition of an older step-brother obviously was not going to push this child out of his rightful place in his family.

As the children watch their family's membership drastically change, they become very aware that the family they are currently a part of may not be the one they will be part of in the future. This creates a relatively insecure environment, as the children realize that the composition of their family can change in an instant, without their feelings being taken into consideration, yet again. There is also a problem for adults and children in communities where there is more than one family bearing their own father's name. Sometimes it is hard to figure out who is currently married, and who is formerly married, to the same man.

There were once three Mrs. G's, all members of the same country club, who at one time or other had been married to the same Mr. G. It got so confusing for the maitre d' at the club to keep track of where they were seated in the dining room, he resorted to seating them at adjacent tables. Finally, the problem was resolved when the second Mrs. G died. For major holidays and family celebrations, Mr. G, the current and the first Mrs. G., along with their children, spouses and grandchildren, started having dinner together. The perfect example of a successful divorce, by the way. No wonder the postal service keeps asking for increases.

Thank goodness no one can take away the father's right to have his children keep his name, as long as he continues performing his parental role by taking an interest in his children's welfare and keeping his child support current. Score one for the fathers who seem to be shortchanged in every other regard.

Even if, as a maternal grandmother or grandfather, your grandchildren will not share your name, always give your grandchildren the respect of identifying them correctly. Be careful when you are tempted to put initials on anything, or address mail or presents to them. They will notice. So when you introduce them to your friends, please take care.

There will be plenty of missteps as you tread the path through your child's divorce. No one is perfect, not even grandparents. Can you repair some of those mistakes you may have made in the beginning, harmful words you have said, or even harmful things you may have done? Thankfully the answer is yes—that is, except one.

Don't cut pictures of the other parent out of the family albums. One famous divorced husband, so enraged by his former wife's betrayal, commissioned an artist to paint her out of a family portrait. In the ex-wife's space, the artist placed a tree. The problem with such extremes is that it deprives the children of divorce from getting a glimpse of what it was like when they lived with both parents. Some of them, sadly, will have been just too young at the time their parents divorced to be able to remember for themselves.

Rule Three:
Do No Harm

Rule Four:

Slay the Dragon

"It does not do to leave a live dragon out of your calculations, if you live near him," said J.R.R. Tolkien in *The Hobbit*. The same thing could be said to anyone going through a divorce.

As I watched my child and grandchildren dealing with the process and effects of THE DIVORCE, I became acquainted with a dreadful fire-breathing dragon, not only living near me, but living inside me. The smoke and fire I felt writhing through my body acted as a constant reminder that grandparents should definitely be included on the list of divorce victims. Maybe at the bottom, but definitely on the list.

I was feeling the same pain as everyone else in my family, the only difference being that I was enduring mine in silence. IT'S NOT ABOUT YOU kept running through my head. I was in so many ways an outsider, with a dragon of doubt and fear coiling and uncoiling inside me. But I had vested dreams in this emotional shambles.

I'll admit it—I couldn't help feeling betrayed by someone whom I had once welcomed into my family, one who had left so much pain in her wake, depriving me of a future with my family intact. No matter what the real cause of the divorce in your family, you will find all of your energy being expended, like mine was, on anger directed toward the one you perceive as hurting your child's family. Fairly or unfairly, you will want to blame your soon to be ex-daughter-in-law or son-in-law for all the pain you are enduring. Don't be surprised if you even hope he or she is suffering too.

There is one problem with that way of thinking. The greatest damage will be done to you, the person expending all that anger, not to your ex-in-law, the intended target of all your rage. If ever there was a time to be careful what you wish for, this is it. You may fanaticize about releasing one of the ten plagues on the offender, but beware: your grandchildren might be the ones overrun with locusts.

Good Days and Bad

There will be good days and bad. The members of your family won't necessarily be on the same emotional schedule you are. So you will need to keep your bad days to yourself. Those days when you can't go through a door without slamming it, or load the dishwasher without one dish landing on the floor in pieces. And oh, pity that poor solicitor who picks that day to call you selling that new TV service. Some days you will find yourself so out of control that you will want to scream and throw things. I must say when I reached that point of uncontrollable rage, I took it to a new high— or actually, a new low. I grabbed for the black sweater my daughter-in-law had been teaching me how to knit, methodically unraveling it until all that was left was a mound of yarn at my feet.

Consider this a warning. That completely out-of-control stage is just when you need to be the most careful. Try not to do anything you will regret later. This is the time to stay away from the phone, the post office, and the family albums, and to avoid an unplanned visit. Instead of venting your emotions to one of your family members, who may be having his or her own bad day, select something safe to release your anger on, preferably stuffed, not human. It is really hard to keep yourself warm when all that is left of your sweater is the yarn.

Always keep in mind that your grandchildren will also have their good and bad days and are entitled to displays of temper and frustration. Watch out and listen for those slammed doors, things thrown across the room, and sibling punches followed tears and by wails for Mom or Dad. Your younger grandchildren will not be as able to express their emotions and understand the cause of their anger as easily as the teenagers, so you will have to be especially sensitive in dealing with the outbursts coming from them. No matter their ages, be there for them, without criticizing them for their lack of control. A good cuddle, their favorite story, and Grandma's special cookies hot from the oven can work wonders.

Remember that your grandchildren are the ones who can be damaged the most by raised voices of angry parents and even the sound of a crying mother behind a closed bedroom door. Ignore those who tell you your grandchildren are going to get through the family divorce unscathed. "They will adjust, it will just take time," some people might tell you. Don't listen. Just be vigilant for the unexpected blow-ups and stand by, ready to teach them some techniques for dealing with their emotions. Grandfathers and grandmothers may have different ones. It doesn't matter. It only matters that you pass them on to your grandchildren so they are equipped when the next emotional outburst occurs or when they feel helpless or overwhelmed.

I have my own personal favorites. Take your grandchild out for a walk around the block, demonstrating to him or her what you do when you are really angry or scared. It's a good way to demonstrate that physical activity of any kind helps relieve some of that aggressive energy. Explain that those conversations you have in your head with the person who is upsetting you can make you feel better by the time you get back home. Let your grandchildren know you can have really wonderful talks in front of your mirror, too, until things look a little clearer. Be sure to warn them that those sessions in front of the mirror may end up with them laughing at how ridiculous they look when they are angry or sad. Suggest they learn to go someplace they feel comfortable in to cool off, listen to some music, or take a nice comforting time in the tub or shower.

With your smallest grandchildren, grandmothers and grand-fathers can show them the crayon technique. Each of you with a crayon in hand and paper in front of you, draw a picture of what your mad monster looks like. You can share a picture with the children of your personal dragon. Draw pictures of what it looks like to be mad, sad or frightened, and then share pictures of what or who makes you feel that way. You might even get a few giggles out if you draw a picture of their grandfather or grandmother and explain what they do that upsets you.

Besides helping them express their emotions, it is a great way to begin a dialogue on what they can do to make the situation better. My particular favorite way of handling "The Mads" is to sit down and make a list of what is making me so mad, who is the target of my emotion, and best of all, the perfect response I should have given when the mad attack occurred. Of course, if you teach them this technique, explain to your grandchildren that you very rarely come up with the perfect response at the perfect time.

The very last thing I put on my list is what I can do now to make myself feel better. Explain to your grandchildren that it sometimes includes realizing you were partly to blame. One of the sweetest things I ever got from one of my sons when he was very little was an apology note for something he had done that he had thought better of later. It made me laugh because I remembered writing a very similar letter to my mom after I spilled a pan of hot taffy all over the kitchen floor.

Your grandchildren hear and see everything. They know much more than you think they do. Just because they don't say anything, remember that they feel everything, regardless of their ages. If you get upset, they are going to be recording your reactions, along with what triggers the upset. They might not see your dragon, but they definitely will feel his breath. They are looking for guidance, trying to understand what they should worry about and what isn't really important.

Using the Rage

Let me tell you about rage. It took a little time to build up steam. First I felt so sad and scared, I completely shut down. All I wanted to do was sleep so I could block out everything. But sleep wasn't the solution, because I started having angry dreams from which I woke up in mid-scream. The phone would ring and I would answer it with an unwelcoming response. I couldn't get through the day without snapping at everyone I came in contact with.

At first I used all my rage defensively, masking all my hurt and sadness. If I was angry, I kept telling myself, I wouldn't cry. It kept reminding me of the time after my husband died, when the energy generated by my anger kept me alive. The energy got me up in the morning, and it kept me going through the day. The nighttime, when I was alone, was the only time I let my defenses down, the only time I would let myself cry. In the middle of the night I would wake up in mid-anxiety attack, so frightened by what was ahead, a weight lying so heavy on my chest, I didn't know how I would be able to draw my next breath, or even if I wanted to.

With my son's marriage ending, I knew the rage might relieve some of the pain temporarily, but if I let that anger consume me now, how could I offer a hand to help my child and grandchildren climb out of the divorce debris? Divorce, like the loss of my husband, is like a hurricane. It pushes everything off its foundation. The dangerous waters rise until the storm has passed and the water level finally begins to recede. My goal had to be survival, including tossing out a life preserver to those of my family who were not strong swimmers, helping them to reach dry ground.

I know I share the same goal with every grandmother and grandfather: the need to help our family go through the divorce with the least damaging effects. It might help us all to reach our goal if we realize that a dragon has claimed unwelcome residency within us, and to acknowledge the extra effort we will need to evict him. Be assured, your dragon won't hurt you unless you feed him. But if you feed him with your rage, he will consume you. Eventually you will realize that the dragon is really there to protect you against all the hurt and pain. Once you finally let yourself feel the pain and sadness, your dragon will get bored and eventually go elsewhere.

To quote Nietzsche, "The man who fights too long against dragons becomes a dragon himself." Take a good, long look at your dragon. Does it remind you of anyone? Your mother-in-law, that professor that used to scare you every time he looked in your direction, or even your soon to be ex-child- in-law? It is always easier to deal with your demon on a first-name basis, so this would be a perfect time for you to name yours. I named mine after a family joke of my husband's. After all, how threatening could a dragon be by the name of Melllllvin?

Start eviction proceedings on your dragon by working on getting control of your negative emotions. Calm, subdue and wrestle those vindictive and self-destructive thoughts. You know those thoughts—the ones about strangling the focus of your anger. There is nothing wrong with having the fantasy; it is acting it out that can lead to trouble. Instead of a voodoo doll, get a pincushion, preferably big and red. I still have mine, pinned and pummeled. Anger has forced them out of shape, contorted by my first attacks of rage. They sit still, useless, savaged and cast aside. Finally, I turned to needlepoint. There was something about sticking a needle in and out of a canvas that helped soothe me. For grandfathers who are looking for a manlier outlet, go get your hammer and some nails and start building something.

Feeling the Hurt and Fear

It took time, but finally I could look at *what* was really hurting me about the divorce, rather than *who*. What I found was that I was most concerned about maintaining my place in my grandchildren's lives, especially because I was the mother of the non-custodial parent. Non-custodial grandparents are at a recognized disadvantage when it comes to remaining close to their grandchildren, because their ex-in-law child is with them most of the time. It requires a good deal of walking on eggshells to have any kind of contact with them when they are not in your child's care. You might have to just be satisfied with developing as close a relationship as possible when they are with your child.

Working on retaining my place in my grandchildren's life was important to me, especially because I was so far away. I knew I was never going to rid myself of all my anger; it seemed to come and go like those unexpected thunderstorms of summer, but learning how to control it would prove invaluable. It is one thing to talk about getting control, but like anything worthwhile, it took a lot of work to actually achieve it.

It was time to face my greatest fear head on. My grandchildren would have the greatest opportunity to be with their other grandparents the majority of the time. Their relationship could be reinforced by daily or weekly phone calls, babysitting times, and trips to see them. After all, their distance away by car could be counted in hours, but mine by days. And there was a grandfather and grandmother on that side of the family. I was alone and not only geographically handicapped, but physically handicapped too. I was so worried my grandsons would forget me or, even worse, think I had forgotten them. What kind of influence could I have on them if I only saw them once or twice a year? I would have to find a way, eventually recruiting my son when I could to help.

It isn't surprising that the first year of separation and divorce will certainly be the hardest. Never has the unconditional love of parents, also in their role of grandparents, been more needed than during the beginning stages of your child's divorce. If you are in control of your emotions, you will be available to help your child deal with his or her own. Your child has every right to be furious when the full force of his or her spouse's betrayal or rejection finally hits. What is causing the most pain is the final realization that the relationship he or she has put so much effort and time into is now slipping away. Is it any wonder your child is furious? Help your daughter or son get control of his or her dragon too, so your child's mind will be clear enough to make the rational decisions that have to be made.

Divorce is a process, taking place over a lifetime, but in the very beginning, the most drastic changes must be made: choice of home, attorney, and always, the burdensome economic considerations. If your child is controlled by emotion when the important decisions are made, it can prove unnecessarily costly, both financially and emotionally. Help your child, and yourself, find constructive ways to express those feelings of hurt, disappointment and loss.

To prevent my extreme emotions from slowly taking their toll on me from within, I knew I needed to stay focused on my primary objective: helping my child and grandchildren. I started by reading everything I could get my hands on regarding what could be done to mitigate the detrimental effects of the divorce on children. My son focused his own attention on re-establishing his home in a different location, a place where his sons could feel very much at home.

Tips on Handling Emotion

One successful way I used to handle my emotions was to sit down at my computer and write a letter to the target of my anger. In the letter I put down all my feelings. My fears concerning my child's separation from my grandsons poured over the page. I vented, ranted and railed about what I thought was the unfair position of a non-custodial parent. I typed everything on the page that was bothering me. When I finished it, I read it over as if that letter were addressed to me. Then I analyzed if there were any parts of the letter that hurt my feelings, or that made me angrier after I read it.

I tried to rewrite the parts I didn't like so I could say them in a more positive way. My first reaction was that what I had said was not entirely fair, so I changed it. I re-wrote it, striving for honesty so

I would burn no bridges behind me. I was determined to do nothing that would jeopardize achieving a continuing relationship with my grandchildren.

And then when I was ready, I reached out with my left hand to print it out, but my right hand was faster and pressed "delete" instead. All of a sudden, I felt like I had spent the day at a spa. Releasing all that steam and venom from my system made me feel like I had lost a hundred-pound weight from my shoulders.

By this time, I hope you have written your own letter. Once you have the letter just the way you want it, you have three choices: don't mail the letter, don't send an e-mail, and either save it to be read another day, delete it, or best, destroy it as I did. Whatever you do, DON'T MAIL IT! Writing this letter is only an exercise in objectivity, a way to help you take a step back and see the situation from two different points of view. If you want to know what I did instead of mailing the letter, well, you're reading it.

Divorce depends on how you view it. Viewed as a disaster, it will become a self-fulfilling prophecy. How you help your grandchildren deal with the family divorce is critical. If you act as if it is the end of the world, your grandchildren will too. Viewing it, instead, as one of life's obstacles to climb or go around will help your grandchildren relax and get ready for the adventure.

Your grandchildren, in their insecurity and fear, will be closely observing each of their parents and the other members of the family, including their grandparents. They will be watching actions and reactions to everything that is occurring around them. How their parents and grandparents deal with each problem that arises will be the examples that influence your grandchildren's actions in the future. Your grandchildren will be very sensitive to how you, their parents, and their siblings handle their emotions.

They will be most sensitive to the anger and tension created in the contact between their separated parents. If they observe one or both of their parents using their children to get revenge on the other, such as through withheld visitation or child support, it will be viewed as destructive behavior. Children resent being used as a bargaining chip, or as a way to hurt their other parent. They are wise and see what's happening, adding to their own distress.

Focus on the reality of the situation, not on its emotional intensity. Take one thing at a time. Avoid creating scripts of disaster that will just escalate your anger. Try to recognize in what way the changes to your child's life might just benefit him or her later on. Focus on your grandchildren as the reason for practicing diplomacy.

Positive View

Thinking of how this new beginning will give you the chance to really create a better relationship with your child than you had in the past might be a way to overcome your feelings of rage. If or when your child embarks on a new marriage, take the time to develop a successful relationship with your child's new partner, one that will be supportive to your grandchildren. Now you know what to look out for.

As a result of the divorce, I had a problem with my son's girlfriends. I held back from getting too close to them. When I met them, I was friendly, but I wouldn't let myself think of them in any context but the present. When my son broke up with one I was particularly fond of, I had to keep reminding myself, *this isn't about you either*. The relationship had to be right for him and his sons, not for me. I have faith that he will know when it is right. When that time comes, I will be welcoming and loving too. After all, it is a little lonely being the only woman in my family.

To keep a positive view, ignore any criticism you hear against your child, any negative comments, digs or low blows, true or false, as friends and family line up to take sides. If people feel uncomfortable, they seem to say the most insensitive things at the most sensitive times. One phone call in particular almost did me in. It was from a relative who was discussing the pending divorce with me, and she made a remark that immediately produced a fingernail-on-the-blackboard response. "You never know, maybe it's for the best," she said.

It was a good thing there was a great distance between us, because I could hear "Melllvin," the dragon within me, start to roar. With all the control I could muster, I heard myself answer in a voice I could hardly recognize, "It will never be the best again. The best is a two-parent family. From now on, it can only be the best of adequate." Which reminds me, I haven't heard from her since.

Insist on taking the high road, no matter whom you are talking to. Refuse to engage, or your emotions will be ignited as mine were. Whatever you do, keep from saying anything that can come back and harm you later, anything that can keep you from being allowed to visit with your grandchildren. Avoid comments like "I told you not to marry him or her," or "I knew all along it wouldn't last," or the one that causes the most damage, "I knew of the affair, but I didn't want to hurt you." You never know if the couple might reunite, temporarily or permanently, even after the divorce is final.

Avoid Confrontation

Keep conflict at a manageable level. If you avoid adding oxygen to the fire, there will be nowhere for it to go, and it will extinguish itself. If you need to reply to a letter, phone call, or message that has the ability to ignite your fire, don't be afraid to disengage by asking for time to consider your reply. Delaying your reply when you are angry will protect you from saying anything that will come back later to haunt you.

Don't let any actions of the other parent intimidate you. Try to use appropriate humor to defuse the situation. If the other parent says something you know is not true, do not try to dispute the statement just to win an argument. Instead, change the subject.

Avoid confrontation whenever you can. If you are in a situation where you feel yourself "losing it," about to start yelling, force yourself to use a very calm voice, even if it sounds contrived, until you gain control. Get yourself out of the heat of the kitchen and to a safer place. You don't have to stomp off in a huff. Just remember that forgotten friend in the hospital. At a grandparent's age, there will always be some friend or another in the hospital. You can also offer to take your grandchildren to the park, or out for ice cream, anywhere where you can go to cool off. Learn your hot buttons. Avoid letting anyone push them. Divorce is a marriage breaking up; it doesn't have to be you self-destructing too.

In order to achieve a goal with your ex-in-law, such as taking your grandchildren for a weekend sleepover, or spending a set time with them every week when they are not with your child, express what you want directly, in a helpful way that will be received by your grandchildren's other parent as positive and non-threatening. Communicate your request in a way that indicates you are doing something for your grandchildren's other parent, rather than he or she doing a favor for you. Taking the high road around all the pitfalls and roadblocks is not easy—it may in fact be the hardest and longest road of all—but it will lead you to where you are trying to go.

Set your limits early as to what you will do and what kind of behavior you will tolerate. Whatever you do, don't allow yourself to feel that you are being used or not respected; your dragon feeds on those kinds of feelings.

Anger is actually suppressed hurt, so as you fight to control it, you need to allow yourself to experience the sadness and adjust to the loss that the divorce creates. Use the fear of the future to motivate yourself into acknowledging the importance of your goal: helping your grandchildren adjust as well as possible. Fear is resistance to the unknown. Write down the things you are the most frightened about. By mourning your loss, you can face your fears and accept that there is some kind of future. Live your life as fully as possible. Doing things for your family while they are making their own readjustment may help you with your own.

Put It in Neutral

Avoid playing the blame game. Blame is the hardest thing to control. The one responsible for initiating the divorce will find justifiable reasons, directed at his or her spouse, to vindicate his or her own sense of wrongdoing. Each person involved will develop an account of the breakup, and even you as a grandparent will develop your own version. Every perceived bad habit, manipulation, and annoying event that you may have tolerated in the past will now become highlighted and intolerable.

If you find yourself on the side of the wronged, you may find those reasons hard to take, maybe even unbelievable. I am sure your child will have his or her own reasons and blame to throw around. Certainly anything said against your perfect child will definitely hurt. Whatever the reasons, they will never seem adequate enough to cause the breakup of the very foundation of your child's family, as well as yours. At this point you may not only be tempted to assign blame to the other parent, but to your own child as well. This is when the dragon is at his most dangerous. Take a step back. Try to view the situation with as much forgiveness and compassion for both sides as you can.

Practice taking all of the information anyone passes on to you without reaction. Dealing well with those things that bother you is the best revenge. You can't beat neutral. If someone hurts you, you don't have to forget it, or act as if it doesn't matter. The best revenge is having that person see that it doesn't matter. Stop letting it be important. As Ghandi once said, "No one can hurt me without my permission."

Call on your support system. Speak to a sibling, relative or friend who has gone through his or her own child's divorce and maintains a good relationship with his or her grandchildren. Even speak to someone who has gone through a bad divorce to find out how to avoid what they experienced. If you are still having a bad time dealing with the sense of rage, or the circumstances of the divorce seem to be spiraling out of control, seek help. Turn to a spiritual advisor or a therapist who understands the emotional toll that divorce in the family can exact on grandparents. Find an advisor who can guide you through the minefields.

Reclaim the Blessings

Recall times when you were all together as a family. It wasn't all bad, so focusing on the shared history and the blessings of the marriage, your grandchildren, can form a basis for forgiveness. The grief over losing the good parts of the failed marriage is probably what is making you so angry. But be selfish for a moment. It is better for your own health and well-being to get over it.

Once you have learned ways to control your anger, it is time to make friends with your dragon, or at least find a way to keep him caged. First, use your newfound knowledge to understand the situations which make you feel the most aggravated. Try to avoid them whenever possible. Keep the places where you make contact with the other parent the places where you feel in the greatest control. Stick to neutral places like parks, the library, the children's schools, or your grandchildren's favorite restaurant.

If you consciously work on keeping communication lines open with the other parent, limited as they may be, it will make it easier to keep yourself in control whenever you have to be with him or her. Communication is definitely the key. You may find that the other parent is not receptive to your attempts at communication. You will have to accept that for the time being. But it doesn't mean that you have to imitate his or her lack of response. Perhaps you are more comfortable in your recovery than this person. Perhaps it's a chance for compassion and, later, a reaching out.

You can prevent yourself from being isolated from your grandchildren by keeping yourself mentally open to any communication attempts coming your way from the other side. If at the time of the first glimmer of détente, you find your ability to keep your emotions in control is limited, you will get by if you force yourself to resort to what I refer to as "SIC" (Superficial Imperious Civility) behavior. You may not feel entirely comfortable resorting to behavior that you feel is forced and insincere, but it may be the only way to get through the initial unpleasant contact.

One thing you must always keep in mind: divorce does not mark the end of your having to deal with your child and his or her former spouse. On the contrary, in order to share fully in all facets of your grandchildren's lives, you are going to be forced to deal with the other parent, and his or her family, for the rest of your life.

The Withhold Game

Some grandparents make the choice of refusing to be in the company of the other side of their grandchildren's family, or even with their own family if their own ex-spouse is present. They are playing the Withhold Game, but there is only one player and there is nothing to win. One of my oldest friends was the world's undefeated champion at the game. She divorced years before she had grandchildren. Once her two precious grandchildren were born, she never missed her special weekly time with them.

One day, quite disturbed, she told me what had happened the day before with her six-year-old granddaughter. The six-year-old had turned to her and said, "Grandma, I am very hurt when you won't come to my birthday party or school events just because Grandpa is there." No doubt she had recently been taught how to deliver "I" messages. This little girl had learned her lessons well, but sadly, her grandmother had not. She died before she could slay her own dragon and learn the benefits of putting her grandchildren first. What this story tells us is that there are other unacknowledged victims of divorce. Not just the grandparents and the children of divorce, but their children as well.

The grandparents who keep themselves open to participating and socializing with the other side of their grandchildren's family, or their exes, at team sports, holidays, birthdays, grandparents' days, graduations and weddings will be the ones who are always found enjoying the family events in the future.

Slaying the Dragon

Cooperation is really needed by all the parties to the divorce, the parents and the grandparents on both sides, in order to do what is in your grandchildren's best interest. Cooperation is like trust. It has to be built slowly. It is all about helping your grandchildren to be able to love both parents and both sets of grandparents. It takes hard work to achieve cooperation between all the family members after the divorce. It is not an easy thing to accomplish. It is important for your grandchildren to see that they are worth all the effort both sides of their family are exerting. They see the genuine concern to make sure that everything works out the best for them.

You have to want to slay your dragon. It will not die on its own. It is time for acceptance and forgiveness, not to benefit anyone else, but rather, to make it easier for you to deal with what lies ahead. Identify the weaknesses of everyone involved in the divorce. You know they have them and what they are—those things during the marriage you kept trying to overlook. Understanding their weaknesses, their insecurities, their hot buttons, will help in your interactions with them. Also, whichever side you are on—the side that wanted the divorce or the side that had to deal with the effects of it—acceptance and forgiveness is the one thing that will help you survive and succeed in slaying the dragon and putting down your sword.

Finally, embrace the fact that you can never become divorced from your grandchildren. Accept the fact that although your child is divorcing his or her spouse, it does not mean that you or your child will ever be free of that spouse or his or her family. You are permanently bound together by your grandchildren's love. Accept that, once the divorce has been granted, and for as long as they both shall live, the ex-spouses will be inextricably bound together by their offspring and the children that follow.

"So comes snow after the fire, and even dragons have their ending." –J.R.R. Tolkien

Rule Four:
Slay the Dragon

Cooperation and focusing on the children's welfare are the only things that will keep the powers that be at bay. Doing that requires the death of the dragon and the ability to control anger.

Rule Five:

Blood Is Thicker Than Marriage

There is a saying that certainly applies to your child's divorce: "Grandparents are only as happy as their unhappiest child." But there is another saying that might seem appropriate: "Blood is thicker than marriage."

When your child informs you of his or her pending divorce, that child is really sounding the warning trumpets to assemble the troops. This is the time when battle lines have been drawn, and your child expects you to be standing under the flag bearing your family crest. If you have had a close relationship with your child up to now, he or she will count on your loyalty. If your relationship with your child has not been as strong as you desire, than this is definitely the time to do everything you can to make your bond stronger. Your child is looking for you to be by his or her side, both parents giving total support and unconditional love. Never has your child needed it more.

Standing By Your Child

Some people suggested to me that grandparents should not take sides in their child's divorce. But that is not only unreasonable, it is unadvisable if you want to keep a good relationship with your child. Grandmothers and grandfathers have to take the side of their own child during divorce. This is one of those life-changing times that their child will never forget or forgive.

Your child is counting on both his or her mother and father to stand up now to protect his or her best interests, wherever and whenever possible. You may not be happy with your child's decision to divorce. But that may be because you do not have a complete picture of everything that went on during their marriage. You need to try to understand the marriage from your child's perspective, and maybe then you will see the need for the divorce. Regardless, your child has a position, and you need to validate it, and most of all accept it. Make the best of your child's side of the story. Help him or her create a new life in which you can be a productive, supportive presence in the days to come.

Let your child know that you support his or her decision. Support him or her whether you think it is the right thing to do or not. This expresses your confidence in your child's ability to make the best possible decisions for his or her own children. Keep your emotions out of the details. If you are asked whether you agree with the decision and you think it is the right thing to do, say so. If you don't agree with it, regardless of what you would do differently, tread softly. Assure your child you will always be there to help wherever you can.

Even if there is now a no-fault divorce system, there are always two sides to every breakup. Don't be too smug if you feel that your child is not at fault. And don't feel too guilty if your child is the perceived offender. You might not have approved of your child's behavior during the marriage, but you are in no way responsible for it. Just acknowledge to what extent your child's actions contributed to the divorce. Don't be judgmental. And do face the reality that now your support and understanding will be needed more than ever. Most important of all, never let your child feel that either grandparent is siding with the other parent. This is a time when your child is looking toward you for support. Without any criticism, always put your child first. There are no exceptions that will be acceptable.

Balancing Act

Some grandparents are going to find it very difficult to take sides in their child's divorce because of the close relationship they have developed with the other parent. They are probably going to try and walk a line down the middle between both sides, trying to keep their relationship going with their child and their former child-in-law too. As altruistic as this position might seem, don't attempt it. In the beginning your own child will have a great deal of trouble with this, believing that you are being disloyal. There will be enough time in the future to develop a new type of relationship. Just be patient.

I had an uncle and aunt who couldn't bear the loss of their son's wife from their family. She had not produced a grandchild, but she had formed a bond so strong with her in-laws, they couldn't bear to sever it. They continued their relationship with her months after the divorce, visiting her often at her new home, taking her out for meals, sending her gifts on birthdays, etc. Finally their son could not stand it one minute longer. One night, just as they were finishing their weekly dinner with their son, his mother said how sorry she was that his ex-wife couldn't be there too. He gently replied, "Have you forgotten which one of us is your child? I really need your love, support and loyalty now." Message received and never forgotten.

From the very first announcement of their child's plans for divorce, grandparents are forced to deal with the fracture of their own emotional foundation. As grandparents face their aging future, they rarely consider how their own feelings of security include their child's marriage. That is, until the stability of that marriage is removed. That realization can color their opinions and judgment on the advisability of their child's divorce. While the grandparents are dealing with the reality of their own situation, their child is dealing with all the changes that will be occurring in his or her immediate future.

Divorce takes a great deal of time, energy, and money. It requires many more decisions than expected. It is almost like the time it takes to get over a loved one's dying, but that should not be surprising. The dissolution of a marriage is a death in itself. No matter how you look at it, divorce represents a failure. Your child can't help but feel that he or she is being forced to start life all over again.

Rebooting a Life

This feeling of being forced to start over isn't just because of the pain your child is feeling. It's the loss of trust. It's the loss of a safe haven as the home breaks up. It's the loss of the picture of their future the couple had been in the process of creating. How your child recovers depends on how effectively he or she can deal with his or her emotional reactions to all the intangible losses. Grandparents, this is your opportunity to be supportive, your chance to reassure your child that nothing he or she does in life is a failure, just an opportunity to learn from and grow. There can be a great deal of damage to the other family members, too, if they aren't allowed to feel and express the pain they are all experiencing.

Keep acknowledging how well you think your child is handling all the difficult decisions that he or she has had to make. But if you observe some action your child is about to take which might seem problematic, don't hesitate to speak up with some suggestions on ways the situation could be handled more diplomatically. Just be sure your child understands they are just suggestions and not directives. Even if you are overstepping a little, preventing things from getting out of control will eventually be appreciated. If you don't, you may never forgive yourself if the problems grow and fester, spiraling out of control.

Place on the Bridge

Regardless of how difficult the concept might seem, encourage and support your child in having the best relationship possible with the other parent for the welfare of your grandchildren. Your child might think that is too fantastic to even contemplate, considering all the animosity he or she is probably experiencing during the initial raw, angry phases of the divorce. Even though it might take a great deal of time to achieve, view it as an investment. It could be thought of as a future goal to be considered. While you help your child work toward a good connection with the other parent, you can work to establish a new type of relationship with him or her as well.

No one says you can't continue a relationship with your ex-child, but always remember your own child must come first. Your ex-daughter-in-law or son-in-law is no longer your child. There is no longer a legal connection that binds you. Divorced from your child, your former in-law child is now only your grandchildren's other parent.

This change will require you to create a completely new relationship with this man or woman who used to be not only legally, but emotionally bound to you. Your new relationship will need to include a respect for his or her position as your grandchildren's mother or father and an expectation of his or her respect for yours as the child's grandparent. There is no need for you to protect your daughter-in-law or son in-law any longer. Your job is only to accept his or her position as the other parent of your grandchildren and act accordingly. Remember, the other parent can at times control your access to your grandchildren. A civil relationship is essential.

Can you maintain a relationship with the other parent? Perhaps. Over the objections of your own child, it won't be easy. An explanation that you are only keeping things civil in order to maintain your connection with your grandchildren might suffice. If your child, because of a custody agreement, is having trouble keeping close to his or her children, your connection to the other parent could be a tremendous help in maintaining your child's relationship with his or her kids. Never, however, put yourself in the position to be asked by your child, the other parent, or even your grandchildren to act as a go-between for the parents. Remember what happens to "the messenger" and keep yourself out of the line of fire.

If, in the beginning, all of your attempts at a relationship with the other parent are unsuccessful, take heart. Whatever you do, remain civil and accessible. While you are waiting for the divorce freeze to thaw, you might find that there are members of the other parent's family who do not look at the divorce as a friendship breaker. Treasure them. They are to be nurtured because of their shared relationship to your grandchildren. Be sure to keep your conversation with friendly relatives away from personal matters. Offer yourself as non-threatening, building on past contacts.

Don't let anyone, friend or relative, trash your child, and in turn, never say anything about the other parent that can't be safely overheard by your grandchildren. Anything you say may be taken out of context and telegraphed to the other parent to be used against you. Sadly, divorce calls for seeing good people at their absolute worst. It's a constant reminder that blood is thicker than marriage.

Recognize that your grandchildren bear the toughest burden with the divorce. They find the foundation of their lives cracking, forcing them to balance one parent on each side of the fault line. Don't expect your grandchildren to take sides. They can't! They are forever balanced like a bridge, connecting their two family sides together. A grandparent's biggest role is to help his or her grandchildren keep the foundation on their side of the bridge strong. The grandparent must always be there for his or her grandchildren in any way possible. When grandparents are with their grandchildren, they need to remain open and non-judgmental and keep any criticism or hostility toward the other parent to themselves. It is a time for loving and nurturing the grandchildren as only grandparents can.

Grandma, Are You and Grandpa Steps, Too?

As serial monogamy takes root in the modern family structure, grandparents may have to adjust to serial sons- and daughters-in-law. However, they may want to draw the line at sharing their grandparenting role with their child's stepchildren who have living grandparents of their own. Certainly, the grandparents can choose to develop a new kind of relationship with any other children that have been added to their child's home, but it can and should be a different kind of relationship than they have with their own grandchildren. Grandparents should be the one relationship your grandchildren should never be forced to share, an unbreakable, unique bond. In addition, as people live longer, a new living generation of great-grandparents has developed. This generation also has to adjust to these new family mixes. They are new players added to the family.

The effects of the changes that families are going through are the most obvious during the celebration of holidays and other family occasions. It is often up to the grandparents to weave the various parts of these new millennium families into something that resembles a whole. Even if the grandparents are not too happy about this mix-master family life, they need to participate in its gatherings, keeping their grandchildren's welfare front and center. It requires them to always be civil, even friendly, to make this arrangement run smoothly. If not, it will be the grandparents who are cut out of the mix.

After the divorce, the two sides of the family can get very confusing to both grandchild and grandparent with the introduction of the steps: step-father, step-mother, step-brother and step-sister. "Step" is not a bad word, contrary to what my oldest grandson thought. His father quickly assured him that was not the case; it just means they are only connected by blood to their own parent and siblings, not to the other members of their step-family. I guess the story of "Cinderella" had left its imprint on him. Some people just can't put aside their image of that wicked stepmother.

Parents who are bringing together two separate families might mistakenly think that dropping the identification of "step" can help the various children make the living together as siblings easier. This philosophy only serves to confuse an already confusing situation, especially when adults ignore or minimize their stepfamily identity. This distinction becomes even more important if or when the stepfamily connection ends by divorce. Statistics on stepfamilies as long-lasting are not positive.

I remember sitting at a hot dog stand counter in Beverly Hills one day, when a friend of mine sat down next to me and introduced me to her real estate agent. The woman looked at me and without bothering to introduce herself, said "I was your husband's former stepmother." I guess it was up to me to figure out if she was the first, second, or third stepmother he had had, none of whom had been too wicked.

The remarriage and introduction of the new spouse's children into your grandchild's home can be very disturbing to them at first. Whether they are being forced to fit these siblings into their space, or if they are the ones being forced into some other children's space, it requires a major adjustment. Even accepting a new baby sibling into their home is difficult. How can there be a half-brother or sister, anyhow? The image of a half-sibling may be a little too graphic for their young imaginations, especially at the thought of sharing one.

This is a time when your grandparenting role to genetic or adoptive grandchild becomes clear. When the position of your grandchildren in one of their homes becomes blurred, the grandparents can give the greatest support. The question your grandchildren will surely ask is, "Do grandparents become steps too?" The dictionary definition clarifies the situation: "Related by the remarriage of a parent, not by blood," and of course adoption too. There is no firm and fast rule for grandparents. To be or not to be is really the grandparent's decision. If the stepchildren in the home already have their own grandparents, there is really no reason to add additional grandparents.

Many grandparents are not happy at the thought of sharing their grandchildren with any but the other two genetic grandparents. One of the reasons is simple. They may want to avoid being hurt when the title they so enjoy is usurped by the insensitivity or ignorance of others. For example, a recent school concert featured the grandson of a friend. After the concert, my friend, the grandmother of the performing artist, stood with her ex-husband and his new wife when a parent of one of the other students came over. Looking directly at the grandfather's latest wife, the new arrival enthusiastically said, "You must be so proud of your grandson, he was fantastic." Quickly, without missing a beat, my friend, the grandmother, answered, "Thank you very much. I agree. My grandson was terrific." She had had a lot of prior experience protecting her position.

Not being forced to share their grandparents might also prove beneficial to your grandchildren. Their grandparents will remain the one constant in their lives. Grandchildren appreciate knowing there is someone who will always put them first, someone they can always rely on regardless of their parents' marital relationships, which can change several times during their lives, and the identity of the steps with it. Even after the grandparents' deaths, their connection with their grandchildren will always remain.

Grandparents have a responsibility to make their role very clear. Grandchildren must know they can always rely on their grandparents' loyalty. What is the responsibility of the grandparents to their grandchildren's step-siblings in the home? Everyone can use another grown-up friend in his or her world, right?

Rule Five:
Blood Is Thicker Than Marriage

Your loyalty will be rewarded.

Rule Six

Reinventing Your Relationship

Remember that old Irish saying, "Your son is your son till he takes a wife, but your daughter's your daughter for the rest of her life"? Unless, of course, either is an in-law after a divorce. The loss of an in-law child may not be as hard as losing your own offspring, but it still leaves a feeling very similar to mourning, requiring a considerable period of recovery.

There is one major problem, though. The former in-law child is still around. Now you have to deal with the disappointment, or even worse, the betrayal, associated with him or her. Once a member of your family, this person has gone through an unrecognizable transformation. His or her smile, the one that use to be for you, has become a scowl. His or her voice, which once called you Mom or Dad, has lost its warmth. Overnight this person looks through you with a blank stare, as if you have suddenly become a stranger. Or even worse, he or she turns away from you when you approach. Nothing is the same.

Someone New Again

You will have to force yourself to become acquainted with this new known someone, now casting a shadow of your shared history behind himself or herself. It is time for you to start all over again, reinventing a relationship with this ex-child. Whatever relationship you form with your grandchildren's other parent, from this moment on, like it or not, will be the one you share for the rest of your life. Your child may be able to erase his or her marriage, but the divorce that is forged remains in stone.

One of Each, Plus Four

With the new emphasis on equality in divorce, it has finally been recognized that each child has only one mother and one father. Both need to play a significant role in the child's life. Your grandchildren require both parents, working together, to carry them through the initial crisis of the divorce itself. And their continued respectful co-parenting will provide the children with a stable basis for a healthy and happy future.

Grandparents also have a co-parenting role. It is really helpful if the maternal grandparents and the paternal grandparents work together to develop the best possible relationship with both of their grandchildren's parents. Their cooperation is needed to assist the parents in making co-parenting go smoothly and not have their actions make the adjustment to the divorce even harder than necessary.

Sometimes, because the other parent is so insecure, or bent on revenge, he or she may try to make any attempts at contact by the grandparents on the other side of the family as difficult as possible. It's as if this person thinks the grandparents will eventually give up and go away. If this applies in your case, it may be even harder to keep an uninterrupted relationship with your grandchildren. You may have to accept that you will only have the opportunity to be with your grandchildren, or in contact with them, when your own child has custody. Whatever you do, don't let the fact of the divorce, or the other parent's attitude, get between you and your grandchildren. To accomplish this, it is time to work hard on forgiveness.

When you are with your grandchildren, keep reassuring them that they can love and have a continuing relationship with both parents and their other grandparents without being disloyal. And try to follow your own advice. Demonstrate your willingness and intention to develop a new type of relationship with the other side of the family. When dealing with your counterparts and their child, it is up to you to create a positive attitude that will be non-threatening.

Studies have revealed that because mothers are most often granted the position of custodial parent, paternal grandparents have the hardest job maintaining a close relationship with their grandchildren. But paternal grandparents, don't despair. It doesn't mean that a close relationship is impossible, only that it will require more effort and creativity.

Planning Ahead

To some parents, co-parenting does not come easy. If your child and his or her spouse were disorganized while they were married, they will find that divorce requires them to quickly learn organizational skills. Their co-parenting ability will be tested almost immediately when they are required to work together to create a parenting plan for their children.

Co-parenting means just that: joint decisions. Those decisions concern legal custody, child support, health care, education, visitation schedule, including time and place of exchanges, and even methods of conflict resolution. All of this must be laid out for the year ahead. It is no easy task. Just think how you would feel if you were required to schedule every detail of your life a year ahead. But it will help your grandchildren to know that the parent they are separated from has made plans to be with them in advance. It serves as a first building block between separated parents to build trust and sustain love towards the anxious child.

If your child is the non-custodial parent, encourage him or her to discuss this parenting plan with your grandchildren so they can count on seeing this parent on a regular basis. The need to do this became very evident to me when my son and his older child discussed the times he was scheduled to be with his sons for the coming year. He explained how he wished he could be with him and his brother all the time, but he was required to stick to the parenting plan the court had approved.

"Oh," my grandson replied, "I thought you just didn't want to see us any more than that." Be prepared, and listen carefully. There will be many of those times when your child or grandchild says something you will have trouble hearing over the breaking of your heart.

The parenting plan calendar is actually a good thing for your grandchildren. Since your grandchildren are used to having calendars covering their school and extracurricular activities each year, their parents can simply add parenting time to their children's calendars. It can become routine for your grandchildren to consult the calendar when scheduling their additional activities. It will also make it easier for you to make plans to be with your grandchildren without causing conflicts, and for you airport grandparents to be able to plan your visits in advance to get those lower senior airfares.

Little Eyes Are Watching

Every time their parents have contact, your grandchildren will be carefully watching how they act toward each other. They will use their parents' behavior as an indicator of just how important their children are to them. Grandparents, you too will become subject to the same kind of scrutiny from your grandchildren. They will also be watching and listening to everything you do and say when in contact with their parents. They will also remember any comments you make about the other side of their family. As the old saying goes, "If you don't have anything good to say…"

No one in the family should have the idea that he or she can successfully hide hostility toward the other parent or his or her family. Those little eyes are watching, and their memory record button is on. They are remembering how each member of the family interacts with the others. By your positive example, you are showing them how important they are to you, and that you are making every effort to maintain a relationship with the other part of them.

If you treat the other parent and grandparents with respect, whether that respect is reciprocated or not, your grandchildren will take notice of which behavior is preferable. It is a conscious choice each member of this divorced family will make. Do people harbor all those pent-up, painful emotions and continue to suffer through each family milestone? Or do they put their grandchildren's needs before their own?

Big Brother Joins the Family

In both marriage and divorce, parents share the same thing: the joint responsibility for determining what is in the best interest of their children. There is one difference, however. If after the parents' divorce, one or both parents are not willing to work together to achieve what is best for their children, then they open themselves up to someone new joining the family dynamic: Big Brother, otherwise known as the legal system.

Parents are often surprised when they realize they have let an unwanted entity into their lives, one that not only shares their responsibilities, but whose decisions can supersede theirs. That entity has termed the parents' shared responsibility "joint custody," in which all major decisions concerning education, religion, medical care, etc., are determined by both parents, with one parent being given primary residential custody. It is the first indication of the lifelong relationship they are now required to reinvent, one they cannot terminate by any means.

If your child is doing everything possible to maintain a civil relationship with the other parent, but the other parent remains totally uncooperative, your child may have been unlucky enough to draw an OPFH (other parent from hell). You know the ones. The court system is inundated with them: the other parent whose only objective is his or her own happiness, or worse, making his or her ex suffer as much as possible because of all the pain he or she perceives the ex has caused.

These parents dismiss the other parent as "crazy" and anything he or she wants as "unreasonable." They are out for revenge, often playing the destructive "Withhold Game." The mother may be withholding visitation and/or phone calls, the father withholding child and spousal support. And worst of all, the parent with the residential custody may move the children as far away from the other parent as possible.

In those instances where the parents will not make the effort to get along, family courts are given the task of stepping in to control and reduce the conflict. Some parents are relieved to realize that there is somewhere to go to obtain help with an uncooperative parent. But they soon realize that the help comes with a high price, not only financially, but in the loss of control of their parenting role. In some of the most extreme cases, where the parents are not willing or able to do the job themselves, the court appoints a guardian-ad-litem to represent the interests of the children.

Custody exchanges have gotten so out of control that in some of the most difficult situations, the courts have created areas where a child has to go through a door of one room to the other parent waiting on the other side. Don't be surprised if it sounds like a wartime prisoner exchange. The similarity has not been lost on the courts, where the area of exchange is referred to as the "Demilitarized Zone." Perhaps this area should be referred to as the "Shame Zone."

Some parents have even developed their own type of demilitarized zones. They take their children to the largest parking lot they can find, one parent parking on one side, the other parent on the other. The child then walks all alone between the two, so the parents don't have to see or possibly be forced to communicate with each other. Shame, shame, shame! Don't these parents realize the children are aware, and are humiliated about being handed off like some hazardous toxic waste? It may be the role of the courts to minimize the conflict in these cases, but what about the responsibility of the parents to start conducting themselves as adults? When will the courts start requiring co-divorce parenting courses for these out of control parents, like they do for anger management?

Regardless of how bitter your own child's divorce is in the beginning, both parents will find that in order to avoid the intrusion of Big Brother in their lives, it is necessary to make every effort to reinvent their relationship into one of cooperation. They will find out it's definitely worth the effort.

As the grandparent, you are not required to reinvent your relationship with the other parent after the divorce. But it is in your own and your child's best interest to do so. Even though in most states there are now grandparent visitation laws available to you which recognize the value of continued contact between grandparents and grandchildren, it is best to leave the courts out of it.

If you are deliberately denied access to your grandchildren and left to resort to these laws, you might as well pack your bags, dismiss your attorney and go home and wait for your grandchildren to grow up. The bad feelings that the court process will generate around your grandchildren with the other parent will end up destroying any relationship you hope to maintain with them. Your grandchildren cannot help but side with their parents. To expect anything else is unrealistic. The parent they are living with is the adult they must depend on for all of their needs. Instead of choosing to play your "rights" hand in court, reinventing your own new, positive relationship with the other parent will prove more effective—and definitely less costly.

At the start of the divorce, when control of hostile feelings is weakest, grandparents who are lucky enough to have been allowed access to their grandchildren may be the only acceptable conduits between both parents. They learn quickly that they have joined the Divorce Circus, performing a high wire act by supporting their child on one shoulder, while maintaining a civil relationship with the other parent and his or her family on the other. Opening up civil communication with the other parent might have the effect of improving your relationship with your child as well.

Transformation

This change from in-law child to other parent will not happen immediately. It is going to take time, work, effort, and above all, patience. There is one good thing about the reinvention of this relationship. You are not entering into it blindly. You know a lot more about this person now that he or she has exited your family than you did when he or she first became a part of it. You are familiar with all of this person's foibles, strengths, truths and prevarications.

Now that your in-law child is no longer legally connected to you, except through your grandchildren, you can make a relationship based on who this person actually is, rather than the favorable package he or she presented to you before marrying your child. Concentrate on the things you really admired about the other parent, the positive things that you remember from the marriage. This might help you focus on your goal: to build a more peaceful world for your grandchildren by developing a new relationship with the other parent, to one of a friend or associate.

As you begin to reinvent your new relationship, regardless of your positive attitude, prepare yourself for the probability you will be met with of a lot of resistance or even total rejection. But keep in mind you don't have to be friends, best or otherwise. You are no longer legally related. The only thing you will continue to share are the parenting interests that relate to your grandchildren. And if the other parent has primary custody of your grandchildren, you will find yourself at a disadvantage. You need to go slowly and choose your words carefully.

Since grandparents, by their age alone, possess the greater amount of maturity and wisdom, they are the perfect candidates to extend an olive branch. In the beginning stages of the divorce, the conflict between the parents maybe so intense that the first olive branch extended might be used for kindling and tossed into a fire. But with patience, another can always be extended later when the transformation of the relationship begins to take shape.

Pick your battles very carefully. Find ways to fight them differently. If the other parent is treating you like gum under his or her shoe, practice becoming proficient in the art of "SIC" (Superficial Imperious Civility). Or at least offer a pretense of civility, even if the visions of the head atop the neck you are figuratively wringing have a close resemblance to you-know-who. Grandmothers sometimes have more trouble keeping their emotions under control, so hopefully there is a grandfather around to keep her calm. There are benefits to be gained by maintaining control. The goal is to do everything possible to prevent the custodial parent from coming between the grandparents and their grandchildren.

It would be best if grandparents try to stay away from as much of the conflict as possible. But they should continue to speak with respect to the grandchildren's other parent, even if the respect is not reciprocated or deserved. Grandparents should bide their time until there are indications the slammed door is beginning to open. They will get the sense someone's hand is on the doorknob with the receipt of the first Christmas or Hanukah card. The door has opened a crack when the order form for the grandchildren's yearly school pictures reaches them by e-mail or snail mail. And by the time a grandparent gets an e-mail or actual telephone call for his or her famous chili recipe or directions to that great restaurant the kids like, the door has swung wide open. But even if the door is open, grandparents need to knock before entering.

The first time I ran into my daughter-in-law after the separation was at my grandsons' nursery school. My son had arranged his turn as "Parent of the Day" for my visit. She had just dropped my grandsons off and I, forgetting the circumstances for the moment, gave her my usual hug hello. As we pulled apart, I realized the situation was an awkward one for the both of us. It made me so sad to realize how quickly our once warm, loving feeling for each other had deteriorated. I was going to have to reinvent our relationship, but at that moment, the feeling of loss was so great I realized I didn't know how.

Communicating In Your New Role

The new relationship between you and the other parent involves each of you assuming a new role. It will require you to create new ways of communicating with each other. You no longer have the parental advantage, and the other parent no longer has to play the respectful son- or daughter-in-law role. So your adjustment will require a lot of care and development.

There will be times when communication with the other parent may be necessary. For example, when you need to deliver an emergency message from your child, when you want to arrange a day with your grandchildren, when your grandchild's birthday does not fall during your child's parenting time, or when you sent a gift and you want to make sure it arrived. Think through any tough conversations before starting them. Decide on the message you want to get across, what goals you want to accomplish, and how to do it as gently as possible to avoid triggering a defensive response. Grandmothers usually are better at this kind of communication. But if in your family, Grandpa is a charmer, you might have him take over.

Focus on only a few issues at a time, bringing up the most important one first. This can help reduce any apprehension you might be feeling about communicating with the other parent for the first time after the separation. If it goes badly, you might not get a chance to get to the second issue. Emergency communications should not be a problem if you state the emergency and what response is requested in as few words as possible. If you are calling to set a time to be with your grandchildren, it might make it easier to ask when it might be helpful to the parent for you to take the grandchildren for an outing, pick them up from school or take them to practice, instead of stating a time when you want to be with them.

Those first contacts should be brief, with small talk kept to a minimum. But don't forget to start the conversation with a civil greeting, such as "How are you?" or "It is nice to hear your voice." Try to keep the opening greeting neutral. Don't let the conversation veer off the subject you are covering. Repeat yourself if necessary. It might help to include a ten-second delay in your brain, so you can think before you speak. Choose your words carefully. Take out anything that sounds accusatory. Your goal is always to get your point across in a positive manner.

It is amazing how paying a great deal of attention to semantics actually pays off. Never was the benefit of carefully choosing one's words made clearer to me than when my son was studying Russian in Leningrad in the summer of 1983 and realized his letters were being censored. He was determined to get around the censors, so he quickly learned to write everything in a subtle code with letters reading like this: "I ate in a Russian restaurant the other night and the waitresses were so beautiful, they resembled Sophie Tucker," or "The food was so delicious it tasted just like gourmet Alpo." His best one was about the beautiful Russian architecture that definitely resembled "Skid Row." It taught me an important lesson. If one puts "beautiful" in front of anything, even something distasteful, it comes off smelling like roses.

If the other parent remains unfriendly toward you, no matter what attempts you make to open up lines of communication, or if this other parent appears spoiling for a fight or gets verbally out of control, shut it down. Seeming to give in to an argument will always prove stronger in the long run. You can always revert to that good senior excuse, the funeral you need to get to, or anything that will keep the situation from escalating into a blow-up. No one can argue with you when you refuse to argue back. And they can't hold anything against you if it isn't said. Step back. Let more time pass before you try again.

Whatever the other parent says to you, try not to take it personally. He or she may be suffering with a lot of guilt or embarrassment, or having a hard time emotionally dealing with the divorce. Whatever you do, don't have disagreements in front of or within eavesdropping distance of your grandchildren. Your grandchildren will be tuned into and upset by any type of "warfare" that involves them. So you need to remain calm and polite. Keep your own emotions under wraps in order to help defuse the other parent's rage.

If the other parent avoids sitting down and having a conversation with you, there are other ways to communicate that don't require a one-on-one. Letters are always available. Or in this day of the Internet, e-mail can be your best friend. You have the time to be very careful what you say in an e-mail. Write out a draft and then soften it before you push the send key. But whatever you do, DON'T CAPITALIZE your e-mail to your child or the other parent, like I did. Everything I had written was taken negatively. Who knew! No one ever told this computer novice grandmother that capitalizing your message means you are screaming at the recipient. I just did it to make the type easier to read before my cataract surgery.

In the beginning days, and sometimes years after, some parents won't even speak to the other parent on the phone. They prefer in this day of technology to communicate by the impersonal methods of fax, e-mail, or texting. If you or your child is dealing with this kind of communication with the other parent, then there are ways to use it to your advantage. If you get an angry e-mail you don't like, don't take the bait. Just ignore it. Then send another e-mail until you get the answer you require. Hopefully the other parent will eventually find the benefit of communicating the old-fashioned way, by phone, where the tone of voice gives you the true feelings behind the words.

It actually took several years for me to recognize that the reinvention of my relationship with my grandsons' mother had occurred. It took my decision to get past the self-protective response I had every time I came in contact with my ex-child-in-law to achieve a positive result. In this case, it was about me, not her, to create a non-threatening atmosphere that would be comfortable for the both of us.

A few years after the divorce, I flew the two thousand miles for a visit with my grandsons while my son was there to see them. At the weekend soccer game, I got the opportunity to say hello to my ex-daughter-in-law. This time, instead of waiting for her to come to me, I went over and sat down next to her. I realized a shift had occurred in my thinking. Just because I was older, it wasn't necessarily up to her to warm things up between us. It was just as much up to me. My dragon had finally been caged. I realized she shared something very important with me: love for the same two wonderful boys. We were in fact rooting for the same team.

I recognized we had both succeeded in reinventing our relationship when she introduced me to some of the other soccer parents as her former mother-in-law. I was thrilled. You see, if the change had not occurred, she would have introduced me as her former husband's mother, as proof no relationship between us had ever existed. Or like in past years, she wouldn't have introduced me at all. Such is the importance of semantics.

Co-Grandparenting

Relationship problems with and between co-grandparents can be just as stressful and difficult as those experienced by the wounded ex-mates. But it must be remembered that every grandchild has the right to two parents and two sets of grandparents, as well as aunts and uncles and cousins too. No one has the right to try and separate them from their family on either side. You might as well demonstrate a generous form of sharing and work together to achieve a supportive environment. You are all members of the oldest generation, and your examples of cooperation are the ones that your grandchildren will look to.

Get to know the other grandparents, if you don't know them well already. If you had a relationship with them before the divorce, try to maintain it on the basis that they are in the same situation you are, grandparents to your grandchildren. Keep in contact with them and do not be judgmental about the way they play their grandparent role, or how they handled the divorce.

The parents of the custodial parent may be perceived by the other grandparents as having the home court advantage, having much greater access to the their grandchildren. Hopefully the custodial grandparents will recognize this is true and show a generosity of spirit to their counterparts. If you are the non-custodial grandparent, try to keep that green monster under control. It will work against developing a positive relationship. Also avoid anything that will even hint at a "Giving War" between you and the other grandparents. Your grandchildren will not respond well to the stress created by it.

It is very important to reduce conflict between the two families as quickly as possible. The higher the level of conflict, the greater the negative effect on your grandchildren. They will be the family elephants, remembering everything—the slights, the insults, the anger and the hurt—no matter how young they are or how long they live.

Remember, you have no control over any side of the family but your own. Continuing a meaningful communication with your grandchildren's other family is not for your comfort, but for your grandchildren's. If the other grandparents won't speak to you or your child, don't give up or act angry or hurt. Keep acting as friendly as possible. Send them cards to say hello, or send pictures of your shared grandchildren. Or you could send a letter to break the ice. An olive branch is always worth the try. Just don't do it by e-mail. It is not intimate enough.

If despite of all your efforts, you still are met with a wall of silence, step back and wait. Always keep the door of the relationship open, and always speak well of your grandchildren's other grandparents when you are with them. If you are the one who has chosen to remain silent, rethink your position. The longer your behavior of silence continues, the harder it will be for you to join together with the members of the other parent's family in the future. This is something your grandchildren will definitely be aware of and will feel powerless to correct.

Grandparents who are not willing to interact with all the members of their grandchildren's family are depriving themselves. If they won't join in the happy times of their grandchildren because of the presence of the other grandparents, or their ex-child, or even their own ex-spouse, they will be the ones who will miss out. Don't give up. Remember, your genes are eternally joined together in an unbreakable bond.

Grandchildren First

There is a joint goal that the parents and grandparents must focus on. The family needs to put the grandchildren first, putting their own interests aside and creating a relatively united front. If the grandchildren feel that all their parents and grandparents love them, that they are committed to getting along together for their benefit, they will relax and work through the problems of growing up as children of divorce.

This is not the best of times for your grandchildren. Their struggle continues as long as their being juggled between these two different families is not made easier by some kind of civil relationship. How well the parents and grandparents cooperate with each other is a definite predictor of how well their children will do. Parents and grandparents need to respect the important role they have been given. They need to appreciate what they are asking of their children. For a parent or grandparent not to recognize this terrific burden that the children of divorce have been forced to bear is to make that burden greater. The goal is to help your child reach the place where the other parent is no longer perceived as a constant threat or monster. Then all of you can work together in the new roles you have created for your grandchildren's benefit.

It is when their two halves, mother and father, and grandparents come together during their children's special occasions that the children in the family will be able to judge how well blended their family really is. They will see how important their parents feel their children are to them. Children have a desperate need to know they are loved by both parents. Children do their best when they have both of their parents actively involved in their daily lives. Add one or more loving grandparent to the mix, and your grandchildren can only blossom.

You will have a relationship with the other parent and grandparents for the rest of your life, so you might as well make it as pleasant as possible. By interacting with kindness and respect, every occasion can be happily shared, and every milestone of your grandchild's life—graduations, birthdays, weddings—can be enjoyed. The more supportive and cooperative a relationship is maintained between both families, the easier the bridge is to cross. And the children will become healthier adults.

Rule Six: *Reinvent Your Relationship*

Reinventing your relationship with the other parent strengthens the two sides of your grandchildren's world.

Rule Seven

Just the Beginning!

Look up the meaning of divorce in a dictionary, and it will say the "ending of a marriage." But every child of divorce understands that definition is not an accurate one. For your grandchildren, divorce marks not the ending but the beginning of a life-defining occurrence, which immediately becomes an integral part of their permanent identity. Ask children of divorce at any age to tell you about themselves. Without fail, the third or fourth sentence will be, "My parents divorced when I was (fill in the age)." Becoming a child of divorce has the potential of inflicting either a positive or negative long-term impact on them. It all depends on their parents' and grandparents' future conduct.

Indelible Effects

As most couples plan to divorce, they are not really looking at the long-term effect that their decision will have on their children. Hopefully, where the children are concerned, there will be some attention paid to making the transition to a one-parent household as comfortable as possible. However, no acknowledgement is usually forthcoming regarding the damage inflicted on the children by the withdrawal of one of their parent's full-time attention, nor to the lifelong burden their children are being asked to carry as a result of the divorce.

In the past there was the thought that most of the damage inflicted on the children was due to what happened in the home prior to the divorce. But the new view recognizes the lasting effects divorce has on the couple's children, forced as they are to experience serious life problems before they reach adulthood. In 1995 therapist Constance Ahrons' book *The Good Divorce* finally focused parents' attention on the necessity of keeping conflict to a minimum if they hoped to minimize the damaging effects the divorce could have on their children.

Undeniably the "good divorce" concept has proven to be a better alternative than all-out warfare, with cooperation between the divorcing parents being the key. But based on the belief that children would be happier in a divorced family, rather than being subjected to the problems experienced in a troubled marriage, it overlooked one incontrovertible fact. Children look at the two-parent family, even the unhappiest ones, as their longed-for norm.

I'll never forget the story told to me by a family court judge about a boy who had been horribly abused by his mother. When the child appeared in court, the judge gently told the child he didn't have to be afraid anymore because he was going to be sent to live with a mommy who would take good care of him. The boy began to cry, calling out for his mother. Startled, the judge said, "But your mother beats you." The boy looked up at the judge and answered, "But she's my mother!"

Even with the so-called "good divorce," the effects of the divorce on the children have not really changed. Parents still divorce for what is best for them, not the children. And the no-fault divorce, or the "good divorce," has only proven to make divorcing easier. The structure of your grandchildren's childhood will still change, but now in a different way. The child of divorce must still deal with the two separate family parts of his or her life, which keep growing wider apart with the passing of time.

Breaking the News

When your grandchildren's parents decide to divorce, they are in effect forcing the divorce on their children too. So one of the hardest times for the parents, leading up to the actual separation, will be sharing their plans with their children. Hopefully the parents will tell the children together, with honesty and compassion. This will be the last time your child and his or her spouse are given the opportunity to demonstrate to their children that they intend to put their children's health and well-being first, and that they will be working together for their welfare in the future. It is also the time when they can do the most lasting damage to their children by demonstrating the opposite. Whatever your grandchildren's ages, this is a moment in their lives they will never forget.

Honesty is the key. Children appreciate honesty, and they will know if information is being withheld. Hopefully their parents will let them know that although the structure of the family as they know it is about to change, the divorce has nothing to do with them. They did nothing to cause the divorce. The biggest mistakes parents make as they head off for divorce court is to assume their little ones don't understand that something is wrong. Divorce affects all of the children in the family, regardless of their ages.

Remember those pre-earthquake tremors as the marriage was disintegrating, with all the stress and tension in the home? The children felt them too. They have a built-in trouble detector, like a seismograph, that records the slightest movement of their world. Children know that something bad is going on in their home, but are often afraid to ask about it. The youngest ones don't know how to ask. Children have incredibly sharp hearing when they want to pick up the low whispers that identify them as coming from a "broken home." Little children, particularly, are very visual. They will be waiting every day for their home to break apart.

For the youngest children, the reason for the divorce is immaterial. They will get the gist of what is happening, probably not asking for an explanation, or an apology, until they are older. If the children involved are old enough, they will probably insist on an explanation right away, although they will be very aware of the dynamics in the family that led up to the split.

Whatever you do, don't allow your grandchildren to be kept in the dark about what is occurring. They deserve to have their parents and grandparents always tell them the truth. Your grandchildren were born not only with built-in seismographs, but with lie detectors as well. Encourage your child to tell the children what is happening, in an age-appropriate manner.

If your grandchildren come to you because their parents have not been up front with them, then tell them the truth. Their mom and dad will be living in different homes. The children will be living with each parent, just not at the same time. And especially, tell them that all the changes that are happening are not a result of anything the children have done. Give them as much information as possible, even if they don't understand it all. Make them feel like they are part of the process, that they are important and their opinion counts. The more they think they are being kept out of the loop, the more insecure they will feel. They will be waiting for the next awful thing to happen.

It is really beneficial to include all the children who are mature enough to handle the information, especially the teenagers, in the decision-making. This gives them the chance to express their requests and suggestions concerning their future living arrangements. In some jurisdictions, the older teenagers are often given the right to decide which parent they prefer to live with. So their parents might as well give their preferences some respect in the beginning, rather than the issue being litigated later on.

Regardless of their ages, all of your grandchildren should be allowed to express their feelings and have their right to those feelings validated. When the children are younger, let them know the decisions that have been made for their living arrangements, their schooling, and the times planned for them to be with each parent. Also let them know how some of these plans can be adjusted as needed and that the children can bring up requests for such changes in the future. This will give your grandchildren a much-needed sense of control. They are learning very early in life that change is the one constant.

Sometimes parents wish to soften the blow, or they feel too guilty to tell the whole truth about the divorce. That is the most sensitive time, because if they make a promise to your grandchildren that can't be delivered, especially a false hope of reconciliation, it can have a severe effect. Children thrive on hope, but they can be severely damaged by disappointment.

Grandparents are usually not included in this important beginning stage of the divorce process. So if you find that your grandchildren were not given the whole truth, but instead one or both of their parents gave them the "I know that whatever makes me happy will make you happy too" speech, you may find that your grandchildren will ask you to help them understand what is happening. If this occurs, answer each of their questions honestly. Your grandchildren should always feel they can trust you to be truthful.

Your grandchildren may also need some assistance in understanding all that new vocabulary they hear being used in conversations around them. Marriage suddenly has a negative connotation, so be prepared to explain the meaning of divorce, especially as it relates to them. It might be helpful if your grandchildren understand how everything regarding their support, care and visitation with the other parent comes under the jurisdiction of a court and judge. My grandsons were so comforted when their father explained that, along with their mother, he was involved in every part of their lives. And he would be sending money every month to pay for their support. My oldest grandson said it made him feel so good that his mom and dad were both acting together to take care of him and his brother all the time.

If your grandchildren ask you to explain to them about courts, judges, child support checks and custody agreements, consider taking them to the nearest courthouse to visit family court. Ask a court bailiff to show them around. It might be a good idea to ask one of the parents to go with you, or at least make sure they approve of this family field trip.

Many states now require parents going through a divorce with children ages 6-17 to complete a Parent Education and Family Stabilization Course before a divorce is granted. One of those courses was developed in Florida by M. Gary Neuman, a psychotherapist, author of the book *Helping Your Kids Cope with Divorce the Sandcastles Way*. His program, called the Sandcastles Program, helps to minimize the emotional impact of divorce on the family.

No, Dear, Mommy and Daddy Aren't Divorcing You

Early in the divorce process, without any period of adjustment, your grandchildren will have to start dealing with the changes caused by their parents' separation. Adjusting to these changes will require a maturity your grandchildren may be years from acquiring, resulting in their having to do a lot of heavy lifting of family responsibility that they are not physically or emotionally prepared for. There may be a change in living arrangements, such as moving from home to an apartment or sharing a bedroom with a sibling for the first time. Perhaps there will be a change of neighborhood, even the change of a town or city. There may be changes in schools, teachers and coaches for the after-school activities. Most critical, they may move far away from their closest friends.

During this time, your grandchildren will be understandably anxious. They will need an explanation for the need for all this change, if not from their parents, then from you. Always avoid a venomous explanation. Instead, the matter-of-fact approach would be best, without emotional emphasis. And always tell the truth. A vague explanation like "Your father has a new job away from us" will be remembered, and if not completely accurate, will return during some inconvenient argument with the child down the road.

Even with the most heartfelt explanation in the world, it shouldn't surprise anyone that your grandchildren might be very angry and confused as they deal with so many unfamiliar emotions. It's possible they will view these changes as something being forced on them. This is where the children's adjustment to losing time with the absent parent is so different from the adjustment to the death of a parent. Here the children realize that the divorce resulted from the choice of one, or both, of their parents. It is no wonder that your grandchildren might appear angry, insecure and fearful about the separation. The nagging question in the back of their mind has to be, "If my parents could divorce each other, couldn't they divorce me too?"

To show how important you think the children's views are, get them around the kitchen table with cookies and milk, or firmly turn off the TV to talk. Demonstrate how important their views are and that they have your full attention. Make it clear to your grandchildren that their parents and their grandparents will never divorce them, that their parents love them and want them to feel free about sharing their feelings with them and any problems they are having.

You might think your youngest grandchildren won't notice, but they will. They will be affected by changes to those familiar sights, sounds and people that formerly made up their small world. The youngest of your grandchildren might not be able to express their views. But it will be very obvious by how close they follow you around that they will respond to all the extra hugs and lap time you can give them.

You won't have too much trouble putting yourself in your grandchildren's place, sharing as you do those feelings of being powerless over what is happening. Your grandchildren will feel out of control as they realize that other people are making life-altering decisions for them. No one is asking them what they want or what they think about the effect these decisions will have on their daily lives.

Children of Divorce Club

While it may seem to your grandchildren that they are the only ones in the world going through this awful disruption in their lives, they have just been granted a non-exclusive, lifetime membership in the Children of Divorce Club—along with the million other children in the United States who join this club each year. Just a few decades ago, children of divorce were considered an oddity, while today fifty percent of children live in divorced homes, each one considering himself or herself an oddity.

You might think that the number of other children going through divorce might make it easier for your grandchildren to accept their parents' divorce. This is not true. Divorce is very personal to each child. Misery may like company, but that company is not welcomed when it comes to your home uninvited.

From the time children are toddlers, they look at their parents as a whole. When that whole divides in two, it has a dividing effect on the child, as well. It's similar to the time when a child first starts to walk. Each parent calls out to the baby to come to him or her from different sides of the room. On wobbly legs, the baby, a little confused, looks from one to the other before making the decision which parent to select. Your grandchildren are going to feel that same confusion. Their world has been literally split in two. They don't know which parent to select. With very little preparation, they will suddenly be thrown into a divided world. Their one family, that has provided them with all their security from the day they were born, will suddenly be separated into two families. This can either be construed as an embarrassment of riches, or as an abundance of tribulations.

When Daddy moves out of the home, because it is usually the husband who does, he won't be coming back to visit the lucky children of divorce. He will be coming to transport them to their new other home. For the unlucky, Daddy will become a hazy memory as the visits become fewer and farther between.

Hence the "good divorce." Now your grandchildren have a chance to live with each parent at different times, leaving neither parent deprived completely. You need to start looking at divorce from your grandchild's perspective, the world of the two homes, "Mommy's House and Daddy's House."

Home Is Where the Heart Is

Where, you might ask, is your grandchildren's home? Remember the expression, "Home is where the heart is." Your grandchildren's hearts have just been split in two. Love from both parents separately is not as nourishing as the love from both as a unit. This is not said to make the divorced parents feel guilty about divorce, but only to force their focus on their children's point of view.

Something positive can be salvaged. The children know they are wanted and loved by both parents. It gives them the opportunity to be involved in each parent's life of family, work, and friends, as well as being exposed to each parent's rules, values, religious beliefs and tastes. Maybe the other parent likes a certain sport, food or vacation, and now the children will have the chance to be exposed to a wider spectrum of experiences. The two separate homes also serve to separate their grandparents from them too. The greatest access, and sometimes the only access the grandparents will have is when their grandchildren are with their child.

Children of divorce definitely benefit from quality alone time with each parent, "alone" being the operative word. This means that no one else is added to the equation until the children are ready for it. If one of your grandchildren doesn't like what is happening in one location, with the addition of new people or developing problems, there is the advantage of having their other home to go to for a little peace from an unpleasant situation. Also, there is another home available for a child of divorce to move to if, once he or she reaches the teen years, the child prefers to live with the other parent until maturity.

However, there is no fast rule as to when a minor child of divorce can choose which parent to live with. It is up to the state the child resides in. Although no state has a law stating a specific age when a child of divorce can request such preference, some states allow an "Affidavit of Preference" to be signed by a child, usually between the age of twelve and seventeen, to be submitted to the court for a ruling. The final decision is made by a judge who takes into consideration not only the age, but the maturity of the child in question and the reason for the request. Sometimes the gender of the child is also put into the equation, since many feel that sons benefit greatly from a close relationship with their fathers in their teenage years. This is not a new concept. In 1943 my husband's parents divorced when he was thirteen. His choice for his father to have custody of both himself and his six-year-old sister became part of the divorce decree.

The unperceived benefit to joint custody, as stated before, has presented an incredible opportunity for the father to develop an even closer relationship with his children than he would have if his marriage had continued. Surprisingly, as he handles all his children's needs on a twenty-four-hour basis, he might just find out that something had previously prevented this closeness. Grandparents, too, might have the pleasure of becoming closer to their grandchildren for the same reason. So they should appreciate that there are actually benefits to the two homes concept.

Now for the negatives. Again, the hardest burden of the two homes, two families, is borne by the children of divorce. Your grandchildren are the ones who will have to develop skills to handle the challenges of being forced to move regularly from one home to the other. Their lives are suddenly subject to the requirements of a joint custody schedule, which when added to an already full school, sports, extracurricular, health care and play dates schedule, can prove daunting to all involved.

Living in two homes requires a lot of extra effort and a lot more adjustment. That doesn't mean it isn't worth it. But sometimes parents can be oblivious to the stress created by the constant transitioning between both parents.

Each time the change is made, your grandchildren may cry, outwardly or inwardly, regardless of their ages, as they go from one parent's arms to the other's. They may subconsciously worry that the parent they leave behind may think that they love the other parent more. Going back and forth isn't stress free. All children miss their parents when they are separated from them, and children of divorce are always separated from one of them.

As children of divorce leave each parent again and again, parents and grandparents need to be aware of the children's feelings of separation and sadness so they can provide the extra TLC they need. With my grandsons, it always seems that the last week, day or hour before parting from one parent to change to the other is always the hardest.

I'll never forget during one of my visits, when because of the long drive ahead of them, the transition was made at 5:00am. Their mother and other grandmother waited in a car out in the still-dark morning in front of my son's house. I waited in the dark by the front door with my arms around my older grandson, while my son carried his sleeping younger son down the stairs from his bedroom. At the last possible moment my grandson kissed me good-bye, turned and, clinging to his dad, walked out of the house to the waiting car. It took hours for me to recover, and I was an adult. The good news is that as the children grow older, their sensitivity to the transitions diminishes.

Other problems you can't possibly expect, however, can crop up, especially if there is a great distance between your grandchildren's two homes. My grandsons' transitions started to change when they were seven and eight. At that age the airlines allowed them to fly between their parents unaccompanied by an adult. The first two trips were thankfully uneventful.

The third trip to their dad, however, was filled with problems from the beginning. The airport they were to depart from was closed because of snow. Their mom drove them to a nearby airport for departure, which meant that their destination had to be changed. But luckily the plane took off, the last one of the day before airports all over the country were closed. Problem averted? Not quite. My grandsons were airborne when their father received the notice of the change. The airport the boys were arriving at was two hours from my son's home, a full hour farther than the original. The flight was only one hour and twenty minutes. Reaching the airport forty-five minutes late, my son ran up to the airline counter asking where he could find his sons. The agent looked as if my son had asked a stupid question. "Your sons," he answered, "can be picked up in Baggage Claims." It is certainly beneficial that one of the skills children of divorce develop early is flexibility.

Friends ask me if I worry about my grandsons traveling alone. Actually, I don't. When I travel I have always watched how caring the flight attendants are to children flying alone. The most memorable time was when I watched a male flight attendant take a girl about eight years old off the plane. When he returned he was livid. He reported to another crew member that it was the first time he had actually been hesitant about turning over a child to a parent. The mother, he said, had not even smiled when the child approached her. There were no kisses, no hugs, no warm words of welcome. "I made her pull out her I.D. and I copied all the information down before I relinquished the little girl to her," he said.

Children of divorce, especially at times of transition, need to be constantly reassured that they are loved and missed when they are away. It helps for them to know that their parents and grandparents will always love them, and are all experiencing a time of sadness and readjustment when they leave one half of their family to go to the other. Each parent and grandparent will always have to accept that there is a part of their children's lives that they are not privy to, the time when they are not together.

Each time a child moves from the home of one parent to the home of the other, he or she must deal with many changes. Different rules and values. A different bed, maybe a bunk in one home, but not in the other. A different view out the bedroom window, and even different stuffed animals with different names and shapes, like Raj and Maggie, on the bed. The most changed of all is the location of the bathroom for those important middle-of-the-night visits, as well as the identity of the parent sleeping in a room in a different location. Anyone who has ever taken a trip out of town and woken up in a strange bedroom, not remembering where he or she is, can relate.

My grandsons also have a different wardrobe in each of their homes. My son feels if they are not required to pack a suitcase every time they change locations, it will increase their feeling of being at home. The only thing they always carry from one home to the other is their original stuffed animals they were given when they were born. My older grandson carries his panda, "Little Bear," and his brother his soft cuddly dog, "Maggie."

What may be the hardest of all, says Elizabeth Marquardt in her book *Between Two Worlds*, "we become insiders and outsiders in each of our parent's worlds." For example, it is wonderful if a child in the family looks just like Mommy or Daddy—until the parents divorce. Then that child is a constant reminder of the absent parent. If the child's last name doesn't match anyone else's in one of the homes, or if the family members practice a different religion or speak a different language in one home versus the other, then there is always the need for adjustment.

Marriage marks the joining of two different family backgrounds into one. The couple works to merge the differences and similarities between them. When the couple become parents, the joined world they have created becomes their child's only reality. After the divorce the former partners no longer have to deal with the other parent's differences. Each becomes single again, living in a different location, with their own individual sets of ideals and goals.

The task of forging one life out of two backgrounds, once belonging to their parents, has been turned over to the children themselves, regardless of their ages. Parents, failing to manage that merger in their marriage by divorcing, somehow expect their children to pick up the challenge without complaint and succeed. This very much necessitates the children of divorce to develop their own identities without too much assistance from the outside.

However, unless both parents and all living grandparents focus on giving the children all the help they need, this is a sure set-up for failure. The negative consequences of divorce on the children are inherent in the divided lives it creates. And they cannot be prevented solely by the efforts of their parents to have a "good divorce."

Their parents' preoccupation with rebuilding new lives, either with a new partner or a new career, can create a very lonely environment for your grandchildren. Sometimes the parents are so distracted with their own adjustment problems to those new jobs and loves that they have less time to devote to helping the children with their adjustment. The parents sometime assume that living in two households, with each parent individually, will not be too different than before. The children are left with the adult job of making sense of their divided identities, long before they are mature and sophisticated enough to do the job. It is like being at a buffet and being asked to select what they want, before they are old enough to carry their own plates.

Keeping the Kids Out of Range

Be on the lookout for how much family warfare your grandchildren are being subjected to after the divorce. This may be the single most important reason that some children adjust to their parents' divorce without too much damage, while others retain deep scars from the dissention they have been or are being exposed to. How the parents relate to each other is the key to why some children do well and others do not.

Some parents are so enraged by each other that they choose to battle over the most insignificant issues, not really understanding the extent to which children are affected by their parents' inability to get along. It is not surprising that some children feel unloved, trapped and suffocated when living in the middle of their parents' battlefield. Since most of the fights seem to be about them, they can get the idea that if they weren't there, their parents wouldn't fight. An insidious guilt trip, self-induced, must be stamped out before it becomes part of their developmental baggage.

Grandparents, you don't need an engraved invitation for this one. If ever there's a time when a grandparent's unconditional love and support is needed most, it is now. Let them know that no divorce decree on earth can ever be granted between you and your grandchildren. Your relationship will last not just for your lifetime, but forever. Be sure to follow through and make yourself available to them as much as possible during this period.

Parental grandfathers have a special role to play in the family with an absent father. The security the male role model provides is much needed by your grandchildren. The grandmother role is very important too. Grandmothers provide extra nurturing in the home of the single mother, and they can fill the nurturing female role in the home where the father has primary custody. In this age of technical advancement, it doesn't matter if you are next door or thousands of miles apart; you can be there for your grandchildren in so many ways.

Shoulder to Cry On

Your grandchildren will learn what children of other single-parent households learned long ago: there are no second opinions available. The decision of the parent in the home is final. The other parent is no longer available in the home to judge the fairness of the custodial parent's decision. And there is no one else to argue for your grandchild on the correctness of that position. If your grandchild feels his or her opinions are discounted, he or she can become a very angry child. This may be a time when your grandchildren seek you out for that shoulder to cry on. Grandparents' shoulders are the best. And don't be afraid to show your grandchildren a few tears of your own.

I know you are interested in what the children are experiencing when they are living with their other parent. But you need to keep your curiosity in check and refrain from interrogating your grandchildren. On the other hand, make time available for them to let you know what emotions they are feeling, or how hard the divorce has been on them. If they are sad, let them cry while you hold them. If they are angry, let them vent while you comfort them. Let them know they can share anything with you, regardless of how painful it is to hear. Tell them they can depend on you to listen to them, without judgment, because you love them unconditionally.

If they don't have a grandmother or grandfather or another nurturing adult to go to, your grandchildren will learn very quickly how to keep negative emotions hidden inside. They'll do this to protect their parents from getting hurt, or to avoid making their parents any more depressed than they already are. Your grandchildren need to feel closely connected with both of their parents, but be aware that they are afraid of doing anything that would risk alienating either one.

As their grandparent, your greatest challenge will be to make sure the smallest children in the family do not get trampled during the divorce process. Develop some mind-reading skills to understand the feelings expressed by children whose vocabulary is not yet developed enough to express themselves like their older siblings do. You may need to wait until the words start to come, one by one, until like a stream they become a flow of thoughts and feelings. Little ones will speak gems at the weirdest times. Maybe right as they fall asleep, after their favorite book. Or while they are on the potty chair, or licking ice cream as it slips slowly down the outside of the cone.

In order to pick up these gems of expression that give clues to the feelings in those very young minds, a grandparent's antennae must always be switched to the on position. Your small grandchildren may not always be able to express their true feelings about the divorce, but give them time and listen hard to what they are actually saying and feeling. Watch for physical signs, like clutching a toy or blankie longer than usual, sitting off by himself and looking off into space, or not being interested in his favorite treat. But the most telling of all is starting to wet the bed again after the child has already been potty trained.

Don't be surprised if your older grandchildren, regardless of their developed vocabulary skills, express their feelings with those favorite one- or two-word answers, like "It sucks!" or "Whatever." These responses are guaranteed to produce a screeching-chalk-on-the-blackboard reaction in all adults. Eventually, if you keep yourself available and your temper in check, your grandchildren will trust you enough to have a conversation with you of real substance. When they finally start to open up, be prepared to field some purely self-involved questions, like "What will happen to our summer family vacations? Where will we have Thanksgiving, Christmas or our Passover Seder? Who will be there for my soccer practice on Saturday?" or "How does a judge decide where I will live when he doesn't even know me?"

Grandchildren might finally feel comfortable enough with their grandparents to ask them questions that plague all children of divorce, but often remain unspoken: "Why did my parents put me in this awful position? Why didn't my parents feel I was important enough to work out their problems and keep our family together? Or at least, why wasn't I considered important enough for them to ask me my opinion before the decision was made?" Plan your answers out carefully, because when the question is finally asked, it will most likely catch you off guard, and it will feel like someone just punched the air out of you.

At one time or another, there is one feeling children of divorce all seem to have in common. They blame themselves for their parents' divorce. Young children's worlds are very small. They imagine they are the axis around which the earth revolves. Their cause and effect ratio is highly focused on them. When something is amiss, they feel that it must be a direct result of something they have done. Children have a secret belief they are omnipotent. When they hear all the arguments involving them, they can't help but think the divorce is their fault. So rev up those listening skills to high in order to pick up any signs of self-blame.

Beware! If children feel responsible for the family's situation, they also can believe if they act up enough, requiring both parents' intervention, they can get them back together. If this self-blame becomes apparent, it might be time to relieve your grandchildren of this perceived responsibility. You can assure them their parents' problems are not ones children can solve.

Your grandchildren never should be asked to take sides in their parents' divorce, or be asked to make decisions that they would not be asked to make if their parents had stayed together. In the beginning, the important decisions, such as which parent will have primary custody, should be reached jointly by the parents. The focus here is to consider where is the best place for the children to reside most of the time. That said, the children should be told that those decisions can be revisited later on. Changes can be made when things start settling down. Here is an avenue of developing trust between child and parents.

Moral Issues and Fairy Tales

One of the heaviest burdens divorce places on the least able to bear it is the moral issues that have contributed to the breakup of the child's world. What makes it even harder is that some of these transgressions involve the Ten Commandments. The children have perhaps been learning in religious school, and implicitly in their parental guidance, what's right and wrong. Now they sense profound contradictions. Childhood is supposed to give children the time to grow up gradually, so that when they finally reach adulthood, they will be ready and able to grasp the meaning of complex moral issues. Children of divorce are forced to deal with these adult issues far too soon. They are forced to grapple with "grown-up" issues, something that can prove very disturbing.

Some parents make the mistake of thinking children are too young to understand. They must have forgotten that their children have heard the story of "Goldilocks and the Three Bears" since they were two or three, and if that tale taught them one thing, it was that finding someone strange in their parent's bed is wrong. And just like the fairy tale will be remembered, to be repeated to their own children, they will grow up to understand all they witnessed.

One mother learned that lesson years after her own divorce, when her teenage daughter surprised her with a question she never expected. "Why didn't Dad help us move when you separated?" Shocked that her daughter even remembered that traumatic day, she hesitated, trying to find the right words to answer such a sensitive question. But her daughter continued, "Dad must have known that your boyfriend was waiting there that day to move in with us. Right?"

From the time children are little, they want to grow up just like their daddy or mommy. This is still possible after some family divorces, if the parents have decided from the very beginning to part on good terms. The children who share these parents are the lucky ones. But sadly, they are in the minority. Parting on good terms is usually possible only when there is very little property to divide or there are no children from the marriage. When there are children, it is almost impossible to part on good terms. For most parents it is very difficult to accept what the divorce will require. The extra financial burden, the difficulty of determining custody issues, and the division of property create a breeding ground for discontent.

The guilt alone for placing such a burden on their children is enough to make that first year of the divorce, at least, a time of constant emotional ups and downs. In order to justify the divorce, each parent intensifies the reasons it was necessary. With this type of "open wound" divorce, parents can become unrecognizable to their own children. The parents' memories are so impaired by pain, they forget the love that united them in the first place. In too many of these cases, one spouse always says to the other when the D-word is uttered, "I never loved you!" That sentence starts more divorce wars than any other. It might take years for a divorced couple to get to a place where the "you" or "me" can be removed from the divorce equation. Only once that is achieved will a "good," successful divorce be possible.

In the beginning weeks and months of separation and divorce, most children of divorce are forced to live in the trenches, right in the middle of the divorce battlefield. Placed in this vulnerable position, nothing will get by them. It is not surprising to find how easily they can be disillusioned. They may suddenly realize one or both of their parents have proven to be the kind of model of adult behavior the children no longer want to emulate. As they find themselves having to deal with the fallout from their parents' behavior, some children of divorce consider one or both of their parents to be hypocritical. It is always hard to watch those you have placed on a pedestal topple over.

Secrets kept by either parent are particularly damaging to the parent-child relationship. Any withheld information will always come out at the most inconvenient time. So keeping children informed about the hard things right away will be easier in the long run. It will save them from losing trust in their parents, as well as enabling them to endure any additional hurt from the effects of the secret itself.

Parents tend to be in denial about the fact that their own negative parental behavior results in damage to their children. It will take time, but hopefully your grandchildren will eventually be able to make their own judgments without the influence of others. They will distinguish right from wrong based on their own observations. And hopefully, they will begin to forgive.

Yearning for an Apology

All children of divorce share an unspoken desire. It's the hope that eventually both parents will accept how devastated their children were by their parents' decision to divorce. They keep waiting for their parents to acknowledge what they as kids have been forced to endure, and what a life-changing event it still is to them. They yearn for an apology.

Because of their feelings of guilt at the thought that their actions could have had such a lasting effect on their children, the parents usually react defensively. They feel that there is nothing to apologize for. The reasons for the divorce had nothing to do with the children. The parents' denial of any responsibility only makes the children's devastation greater. This does not mean the parents are expected to wallow in guilt. It does mean that it will prove easier on them if they accept their responsibility to their children and ask them what they can do to make them feel more secure and supported.

If either of the parents is still letting the guilt get in the way, continuing to dismiss the children's concerns as unimportant, grandparents can be of assistance. Even if your grandchildren are angry or unhappy about what might seem minor to an adult, take their problems seriously. Your grandchildren need you to empathize with them. They want you to validate their feelings and concerns as significant. Ignoring their feelings during this major life-changing period can have a permanently damaging effect on them.

Hidden Feelings, Hidden Fears

Each one of your grandchildren may experience the family divorce differently. Some may never have a problem. But others can suffer at different times and different ages. When problems do occur, the children are going to look for someone to help them deal with what they are going through. If they think that their parents are unavailable to them, either physically or emotionally, they may be the absolutely last people they will reach out for. They will have developed that Richter scale sensitivity about what information they can and cannot share. They hide their sadness so it won't add to their parents' already overloaded plates. They will carefully filter what they are about to say through their sensitivity detector.

Before your grandchildren realize they need to reach out to someone to help them make their situation tolerable, they may need some time and space to try to work through the problems on their own. Give them the time, but, hopefully, after the advice from their BFF (best friend forever) doesn't do the job, they will reach out to an adult who can review the situation more objectively. Grandparents sound like the perfect choice to me, waiting as we are with a shoulder for our grandchildren to lean on, and a friendly ear too, even if it has a hearing aid in it. Assure them you are there for them. You're ready to listen. You're ready to help them deal with any problems that arise. And that you know there will be problems, but that neither one of their parents, or you, wants them ever to think they need to handle them alone.

This is the time when you need to watch out for the smoke signals, subtle signs of unasked questions or as-yet-undeveloped vocabulary. Those signals may reveal themselves through body language, tone of voice, an angry outburst, even periods of sullen silence. In other words, be aware of your grandchild exhibiting any inappropriate or unusual behavior. Whatever the signs, the meanings are all the same: a child looking for someone to help him or her understand what is happening. Grandparents never have to accept a grandchild's bad behavior, but they should try and understand the feelings behind its display. They should let the grandchild know that they intend to be there for him or her, naughty or not.

But there are other signs that parents and grandparents need to look out for that indicate problems that might need attention by professionals. Trouble sleeping, shutting themselves up in their rooms away from the family, excessive use of the computer, uncontrolled outbursts of anger, falling grades at school, and frequent trips to the principal's office are all behaviors crying out for special help. Of course, drug or alcohol abuse or contact with the police are all wake-up calls that can't be ignored.

Be totally approachable, ready and waiting. Your grandchildren won't come to you if you are always lecturing them or finding fault. But they will eventually turn to you if you are with them in an informal, non-threatening way, a time when they can feel especially loved and safe, such as cuddling in bed before bedtime, reading a book, or cooking in the kitchen. When you're driving and looking at the road instead of at them, they may feel less vulnerable.

Whatever you do, when they finally say something of import, listen carefully to the feelings they are expressing. Listen even if what they are saying seems to be in a code of some kind or a roundabout way of getting to the point. If you sense they are struggling to express themselves, avoid being a "Grandparent Interruptus," impatiently trying to complete their thoughts for them.

Simply asking your grandchildren to tell you what they are feeling does not always work. At first your grandchildren may not be to ready to unburden themselves to you. They may be hesitant to share what they are feeling because they fear you will just dismiss their feelings as unimportant or something they will just have to get over. If your grandchildren have already experienced one or both of their parents getting defensive and dismissive every time the subject of the divorce has been broached, they will be even more sensitive.

You will never really know what your grandchildren are thinking. That is, unless you sit down to talk with each one, listening to what he or she is saying, but also watching out for what he or she isn't saying. Sometimes within your grandchildren's comments are unasked questions which they hope someone will "hear" and answer for them. This is when your special grandparent talents come in handy. Try to hear with your heart what your grandchildren are really saying, and understand the questions they are really asking. For that kind of listening you need to give them your undivided attention when you are with them. When they see that you are really avoiding any distractions, like the television or your cell phone, in order to listen to them, they will be more likely to turn to you in the future.

Share with them that they can tell you anything, and that you won't be judgmental, which includes controlling those involuntary raised eyebrows. Be truly present. Listen to what they are saying without offering advice or hooking into their drama. Let them express how they feel, as fully as possible. Mirror back what they are saying so they know that you are really hearing them, get what they are saying, and understand their feelings. Say something like, "You must be feeling really sad or angry because you don't have both your mommy and daddy to tuck you in and read you a story every night. Have you shared with your friends that your parents are getting divorced? Does that make you feel different from your friends?" The answers to these questions will give you some insight into what they are experiencing and thinking.

If your grandchildren are sad, allow them a time to express it. Listen to everything they want to say even if it brings out painful emotions and it makes you both cry. Tears have an ability to make things look clearer after the waterworks are through. Let them know it is understandable if they are experiencing a lot of emotions they may not understand, like anger, confusion and sadness. You might even have to explain to your younger grandchildren what those emotions feel like. Even giving a name to those feelings will make it easier for them to express them.

This is an opportunity for you to teach them by your own example. Emotions are to experience, not to shut away, because once experienced, they are easier to deal with. Sharing your grandchildren's pain, and allowing them to express it openly, is one of the greatest gifts you can give them. It will help them endure with confidence any other great crisis in their lives.

It might be very painful for you and their parents to hear how the children are really feeling about the divorce. But knowing how they feel is the way to help them feel better. I will never forget when I heard my three-year-old grandson say very softly but angrily just as he was falling off to sleep, "Mommies and daddies should live together in the same house." It helped me know that he understood much more than I thought he did.

It reminded me that many years before, I had already learned just how young children can be when they are aware of the problems. One Sunday, when my grandson's daddy was only a year and a half old, a newly divorced friend of ours came over with his four-year-old son. My husband was holding my son on his lap when the little boy came up to him. The boy hesitated a moment and then asked, "Is that your little boy?" "Yes!" my husband answered, introducing them. It was then he asked, "Does he live with you?" No wonder I have been so concerned about mitigating the damaging effects of the divorce on my grandsons. I have never forgotten that little boy.

Always acknowledge and validate the pain your grandchildren are in. It wouldn't hurt to let them know they are not alone, that you too are experiencing some of that pain. At this point, your grandchildren won't be able to understand that they are going to survive their parents' divorce. Early in the divorce they won't be able to see how their parents' living separately will not be as bad as they think it will be, so avoid the temptation to paint a rosy picture of things getting better for them. At this stage, the future does not yet have a rosy glow. Let them know they have a right to be angry, that you're angry too, and maybe you can help each other to get through this hard time.

Remember when you are alone with your grandchildren that they are anxious to know they are being heard. Sometimes it is too easy to dismiss a child's worries, because from an adult perspective, the problem does not appear insurmountable. Don't trivialize their problems. To them they are world-shattering. They are looking to you to empathize with them, to consider them important in your world. Forget those insensitive platitudes like "It's not really as bad as you think," when you know it really is; "Time heals all wounds," when you know it won't; or "Everything's going to be fine," which you know is only a prayer.

Your grandchildren may ask you questions when you least expect them. When they do, they usually will be busy doing some other task and will not look you directly in the eye. When this happens, listen very carefully. They are waiting for you to comment, wanting to know if the subject is open for discussion. They may even ask a question they already know the answer to, testing to see if they can depend upon you for a truthful answer. Once they know they can trust you, they will be more likely to open up to you.

Acknowledge that your grandchildren have an absolute right to ask any question they want and to receive a truthful answer. If they ask for answers about the details that led up to their parents' divorce, give them some guidance on how to ask their parents for the answers they need. If they are hesitant to talk to their parents about a problem, discuss several possible solutions for the problem and how to diplomatically bring them up to their parents. Teach your grandchildren how to find solutions for their own problems. This will help your grandchildren feel more empowered in the future.

If you hear your grandchildren make negative comments about their parents, the divorce, or about something totally out of context, this offers a definite clue to their mood. Take a deep breath. Some of what they say may be completely for shock value. Curb the inclination to return with a retort like, "That isn't a nice thing to say," or "You shouldn't feel that way." The truth is, they may just be testing you to see how you will respond and how truthful you will be with them when you do. Be sure to give them the right to say or feel anything and any way. They are looking for some assurance that they aren't so bad, and are normal to feel the way they do.

Let your grandchildren feel free to discuss their other parent with you, as long as you do not allow them to paint the other parent in a negative light. As you use your two ears to listen carefully to what your grandchildren are sharing with you, determine whether they are really asking for your help, and then give them as objective and unemotional a response as you can. A grandchild might seek out your opinion about their parents and the divorce to try to stir up a pot of trouble. You need to be sure you do not say anything that can't be broadcast to the world. Your grandchildren might be trying to get you to take their side against their parents, but avoid the trap. Never go against your own good judgment just because you want to gain favor with the grandchildren. Remain impartial in a parent-child conflict. It is the only way you can view both sides objectively.

Avoid criticizing the other parent, because children are very bright in these days of DNA. They think if something is wrong with one of their parents, then there must be something wrong with them too. The best role for you to play, if your grandchildren's communication breaks down with one of their parents, is that of a sounding board. This way you can help them restore the connection as quickly as possible.

Try to put yourself in your grandchildren's shoes. How would you feel if you were forced into an adult world too early, wondering why you have to be burdened with such adult issues? For some of your grandchildren, the divorce may be occurring just as they are learning to deal with the world being away from their family, adjusting to school, developing social interaction, and other normal childhood problems. The extra burden adds even more weight on those young shoulders.

Remnants of the Stigma

Regardless of how society's perception of divorce has changed, children of divorce still feel the stigma of divorce with their friends. More children may be sharing the experience with them, but to them, their own family is different from everyone else's. Through their distorted divorce lens, all the other families are seated around the dining room table, parents intact.

The real picture is quite different. Almost fifty percent of the children in the United States have parents divorced or separated. Because children of divorce are so afraid of being different from the other children in their class, they find it very uncomfortable to explain to their friends, teachers and classmates that their parents are divorced and that they only have one parent living at home. They would rather miss parent/child events at school than go through the humiliation of explaining they don't have the requisite parent available.

Keeping what they consider a painful secret prevents them from finding all the other children around them who are in the same situation. It takes time for even their closest friends to learn about what the children are experiencing. They may eventually learn of the divorce, but may have never met their friend's other parent, or in fact known that one exists.

After my sons lost their father in a front-page plane crash, I was shocked to learn, two years later, that my younger son had not yet told his new best friend, or his friend's parents, that his father was dead. I finally realized it and had to inform them myself. What that taught me was that you cannot assume children adjust easily to drastic changes. You have to always keep your eyes and ears open for clues of their unhealthy attempt at secrecy.

Parents and grandparents really need to put extra effort into helping their children deal with situations that make them feel different. It is important to actually check around and find friends for your grandchildren whose parents are divorced too. And if the child has a sleepover at a friend's house, you need to make sure the parents are aware of the situation. It might also be the time to discuss with the child how being around a friend's parents might make the child miss his or her own.

Wouldn't it be wonderful if schools went out of their way to notify the teachers of students who are family challenged? Teachers could schedule a class at the beginning of the term for children to discuss what each of their families looks like, either in pictures or words. It would be so helpful if parents and teachers, anticipating school events that require a missing parent, stepped in to make it easier for the children. They could do this by notifying the other parent to attend, or when there is no other parent, to arrange for an uncle or close family friend or a favorite faculty member to fill in.

When my children went through it, I kept wishing that event organizers would become sensitive to the problem, perhaps making those events open to either parent, but they never did. My sons never were able to attend. I must say that my grandsons' school does make stand-in arrangements for Grandparents' Day. I am hoping other schools are getting more sensitive too.

It might prove helpful to your grandchildren if you look around your area or on the Internet for helpful resources geared to help families dealing with divorce. For example, in California there is Kids Turn.org, a nonprofit organization to help families through parental separation and divorce. They have activities and hot topics all fit for children. They even provide seminars for grandparents. Websites such as grandparents.com or AARP.org are wonderful sites for information on grandparenting. They have free newsletters that provide all types of things for you to do with your grandchildren, along with great recipes you can cook together, special fun activities and trips to go on.

Teens: Special Problems, Special Needs

Since it is normal for teenagers to experience conflict with their parents, having divorced parents only makes the problems more complicated. With only one parent to deal with at a time, it is not unexpected that as an adolescent matures, he or she will begin to act out and rebel. The teen might turn to friends as the final arbitrators of what is right and wrong. Hopefully, teens will eventually learn to turn to someone like a grandparent, whom they respect and who is more experienced, to help them deal with their problems.

Because grandchildren are impressed by the fact that their grandparents raised their own parents, they consider them perfect for the role of arbitrator. What grandparents need to understand is as their grandchildren mature into adolescents and then adults, they need their grandparent to relate to them in a more mature way.

When a teenager's parents divorce, all the love and support the teen has depended upon from his or her parents appears to disintegrate. The child might view this as a personal betrayal. The divorce places adult-type burdens on teens that they are not quite ready to assume, like taking care of their younger siblings and the running of the house when the parent is at work. Their living environment can be so chaotic that it is not conducive to normal adolescent development.

The teenage years are a time when friends take on a more important position in your grandchildren's lives than their parents do. It can create a potential battleground with the other parent when the parenting plan calling for time with the other parent conflicts with a teen's social calendar. Also, when children of divorced parents become teenagers, in most jurisdictions they are allowed to request which parent they wish to live with. So the parents are going to need to work very hard to fit into their teenagers' lives rather than the other way around. It is going to take a lot of respect and understanding between parents and teens to make their time together compatible until the children reach maturity, in hopes of making their adult relationships loving ones.

One of the main problems when the divorce happens is that it is not only the parents who don't understand their teenagers; it is also the teenagers who do not understand their parents. In addition, adolescents in divorced families are often preoccupied and affected by the behavior of their parents. They are concerned about their parents' morality or lack of it. Even the traditional commandment about honoring their parents that all children are taught to follow becomes confusing when they realize their parents have broken some of the very commandments they have expected their children to respect. Teenagers have reached a point where they understand the term "hypocrisy." It's probably presumptuous to want to add a new commandment, but "Respect thy children" or maybe "Honor thy family" might be an acceptable compromise.

Because teenagers are so concerned about being embarrassed in front of their friends, they do not find it easy to talk about what is occurring in their home. A grandparent is the one person that grandchildren may feel they can talk to about their parents without feeling disloyal. Grandparents can relieve some of the burden their grandchildren are carrying. They can act as a sounding board, a counselor and a cheerleader. But they should be reminded that what they say to their grandchildren is not always as important as what the grandchildren say to them. Don't forget, you only have one mouth but two ears. So listen twice as much as you speak.

From toddlers to teens, the children of divorce are too young to carry the burden placed on them alone. They need to know they can call on help from their parents, teachers and grandparents to share the load with them. It's like when a mother returns from the market with her car full of groceries. She makes sure the bags she asks her children to take into the house are never heavier than they are strong enough to carry. Children of divorce need to have the burden of their parents' divorce doled out to them slowly too, until they are ready to carry the whole weight on their own.

Rule Seven:
Just the Beginning!

The burden divorce has placed on your grandchildren has just begun. Help lighten the load.

Rule Eight

As Long As You Both Shall Live

Marriage and divorce are quite similar. Both take two consenting adults, require legal documents, and take a lot of work and dedicated commitment to make them successful. A wedding marks the beginning of a marriage, so perhaps a funeral marks the end of a divorce—with all the relatives and friends still confused as to which side of the aisle they should sit on.

To be successful, both marriage and divorce require the same things: communication, respect, friendship, forgiveness, and the ability to focus on the well-being of someone other than oneself. Those whose marriages contain these components are still married. Those who fail to acquire them in time for a successful marriage still have the potential for achieving a successful divorce.

Without children, divorce marks the end of the marriage. But with children, divorce will last "as long as they both shall live." In other words, divorced-with-children is a permanent, irreversible relationship. Acquiring the skills for a successful divorce will take awhile—perhaps a year, or in the worst scenario, a decade or more. So in the beginning things might not be too good, what with all the emotional ups and downs slowing the achievement of success.

Ignoring the Guilt

Parents are aware that their divorce will create problems for their children. But because a divorce precipitates guilt, that parental awareness is pushed unacknowledged to the backs of their minds. Once parents and children finally sit down and talk about the divorce, they will find that the parents' experiences of the divorce and the children's experiences are not at all similar. It is understandable that parents making plans for their divorce are only concentrating on seeking a more fulfilling life for themselves in the future, not on the ending of the marriage they no longer value. The children, too young to understand what the parents are dealing with, consider the divorce an indication that their parents don't consider them important enough to make an attempt to work through their problems.

Parents, feeling overwhelmed as they do with all the decisions and actions they are forced to deal with, may have less time for giving full attention to their children. Many divorcing parents have to find a new place to live. Some need additional education to become employable, and some need to return to work immediately. For the custodial parent left alone with the children, the biggest adjustment is to the loss of those extra hands in the home and the shoulder to lean on. It is not at all surprising that mothers may feel very vulnerable, and fathers devastated by the separation from their children.

Separating couples, dealing as they are with all the changes necessary, assume that whatever they decide is best for them will just have to be best for their children. Trying to excuse their own behavior, they explain the divorce as their attempt to make all of their lives better. This is something their children will take a long time to accept and may never understand.

Children of divorce might find it tempting, while their parents are so vulnerable, to play the guilt card to the hilt. But that will just elicit a defensive posture from their parents that will not prove beneficial. Parents do feel guilty. They just have trouble owning up to their own mistakes and getting past them. Until they do, the parents will not be ready to be honest and face the effects the divorce has had or will have on their children. Hopefully, they will finally be ready to help their children with their adjustment before too much damage has been done.

It might be a great help to the divorcing couple and the children if the grandparents can step in with a great deal of attention and understanding, to give the children the extra time they need to make the adjustment. Working toward achieving a successful divorce will just have to wait until the parents get past the emotional upheaval of the divorce itself. The only success they can achieve, in the beginning, is to shut out the pain of those around them.

As children of divorce try to share their problems or feelings with their parents, they become too familiar with the common refrain, "Later, I don't have time to talk to you about that now." The parents, so overwhelmed with their own problems, are not able to deal with anyone else's, even their children's. Eventually, if the children feel shut out and alone, they will no longer even try to share anything with their parents.

Hopefully one of their grandparents will be available to listen. Grandsons might prefer their grandfather as their confidant, while granddaughters might feel more comfortable with their grandmother. Regardless, attention from at least one of their grandparents will be welcome.

Anger Payoff

One of the biggest obstacles to achieving a successful divorce is the payoff some divorced parents seem to get by refusing to let go of the anger they direct at their former spouse. It's as if selective memory has eradicated all happier times. They just refuse to slay the dragon. They paint the other parent as the villain in the piece. They blame the breakup on the unwillingness of their ex-spouse to make the marriage work. Sometimes this is true, sometimes not.

It takes effort to let go of all the anger. My mother used to say, "Not letting go of your anger makes about as much sense as hitting your head against the wall and expecting the focus of your anger to get the headache." A parent might find it more effective to expend that energy on achieving a successful divorce.

Children understand at a very early age that they are part of both parents. When one parent badmouths the other, children understand it to mean that something is wrong with their other parent part of themselves. Parents don't intentionally want to hurt their children. The exact opposite is true. But their refusal to let go of their anger ends up being devastating to everyone. Here's a good rule for all grandparents to follow: don't trash the other parent in front of your grandchildren. If you keep the thought that everything is being recorded in your grandchildren's minds, you will know how important it is to keep your opinions as positive as possible.

When a mother creates such negative surroundings for the children in her custody, it is only natural that the children will eventually blame their father for not being around to share the burden with them and to protect them from living in such a hostile environment. Grandparents really need to keep a lookout for any uncomfortable situations created by either parent beginning to affect their grandchildren. If you hear any of your grandchildren saying, "I can't handle that," it is a definite signal that they have been exposed to an overwhelmed parent. You might even pick up indications of your grandchildren's anger as well. This is a call for help. It's a time to step in and help your grandchildren relieve their stress whenever possible, even if you aren't asked.

Alienation

Another thing to watch out for is the escalation of one parent's anger to the point that he or she tries to interfere with the other parent's access to the children. Each divorced parent has the responsibility to encourage an ongoing relationship with the other parent. But a parent bent on revenge, acting out of bitterness and spite, can work to sabotage that relationship. Some parents will tell the other parent their child needs more time to adjust to the separation, or that the child has scheduled activities on that day which make being with the other parent inconvenient. Sometimes those activities have being intentionally scheduled to interfere with the other parent's parenting time.

An angry parent can create such an insecure environment in the home that the children get the sensation of always walking on eggshells. They cry when the other parent takes them, or refuse to go at all, unconsciously thinking that kind of behavior will make the parent they are leaving happier. Sometimes children use compliance to make their daily lives easier, even if the result is to make the children feel abandoned by their absent parent. Regardless of how young the children are, they have learned their first coping mechanism.

In June of 2010, New York judge Robert Ross finally took the action alienated parents all over the country had been praying for. He sentenced a mother to six weekends in jail for her successful attempts at alienating the couple's two daughters from their father. The judge ruled that the mother was in contempt for violating the couple's joint custody agreement. There would be no problem with child care while the mother was in jail, since the time would be served every other weekend in accordance with the father's scheduled parenting time.

Without a judge's intervention, some parents get so upset they react in various unacceptable ways. One famous father unleashed his anger on his daughter's answering machine. The worldwide court of public opinion harshly criticized this frustrated father. The fact that the target of his rage was not his daughter, but the owner of the answering machine was never even considered.

Some husbands and wives become so enraged they resort to much more violent measures. The resulting tragedies are too often reported on the front page of the newspaper or as the lead story on the six o'clock news. Some are so extreme that in 2010 the governor of California signed an amendment to an existing law preventing a spouse found guilty of hiring a hit man to kill his or her spouse from benefiting in any way from that spouse's estate or benefits. It seems that "Slayer Statutes" already on the books in most states, which prevent a husband or wife who kills or attempts to kill his or her spouse from inheriting from the estate, forgot to include hit men (or as referred to in this age of equality, "hired guns"). Regardless, it is important to remember that divorce in some cases is a life and death issue.

Some non-custodial parents are so destroyed by the other parent's interference that they just give up. They mistakenly think that if they stay away, they might actually be relieving some of the extra stress on their children. They might intend to reinitiate a relationship when their children get older. The sad part, however, is the absent parent is taking a risk that when the children are older, they might not forgive the other parent for his or her absence. They might blame that parent for staying away when the children needed him or her most.

It also can have the same effect on a grandparent who stays absent to make it easier on the grandchildren. The grandchild may never forgive the grandparent for being absent during his or her childhood. That was what happened with my husband's maternal grandparents. After his parents' divorce, he never saw his maternal grandfather again. His maternal grandmother showed up once after we were married, in time to meet her great-grandson.

The parent who is indulging in such withholding tactics may think he or she has won some kind of divorce prize by keeping the other parent at bay. But the fact is, this destructive behavior may have succeeded in inflicting permanent damage to the children and creating the "divorce from hell," the complete opposite of a successful divorce.

Some assume that alienation is a female pursuit. That would be wrong. Many fathers who have primary custody practice this spiteful behavior too, adding economic intimidation to the mix. One more subtle approach some custodial parents use is to simply relocate their children, moving them physically away from their other parent. They can easily accomplish this by claiming economic benefits for the move. With a new job given as the reason, courts find it hard to rule against the move, even though it prevents the other parent from seeing the children as frequently and adds the economic burden of travel to the absent parent's already overburdened financial responsibilities.

Grandparents who observe this escalating destructive behavior should not stay silent. Try to remain as objective as possible, but point out how a different type of action might prove effective. If your child is the parent being subjected to this alienating behavior by the other parent, encourage him or her to keep a close relationship with the children. He or she should not allow the other parent to get away with any attempts at interference. Regardless of the extra burden, it will really prove worth it.

If the other parent won't cooperate, it's time to check with the legal representation engaged at the time of divorce to handle the new problems that have developed. If the children have been moved to a different state from where the original divorce was granted, see if the original attorney can refer you to a new attorney. If not, it's time to start the attorney search all over again.

Need for Big Brother

Sometimes, even when the other parent has made every attempt possible to improve the situation, the problems are so insurmountable and the alienation so severe that it is time to get the courts involved. If it is your child that is erecting those road blocks to prevent contact between your grandchildren and the other parent, you might point out just how badly your child's actions could backfire. Constantly being forced into court can prove very costly, as well as time consuming. Also, such alienation can ultimately cost more than your child might be willing to pay: the loss of custody, as well as his or her children's holding the behavior against that parent forever.

There is hope. If the angry parent finally takes himself or herself out of the equation, that parent will realize how important the relationship with two parents is to the children's development. There are rewarding benefits to be gained. Your grandchildren will quickly notice the shift in their parents' behavior. Once they do, they will become aware of just how much weight has been lifted from their load. Finally they will be able to sweep the eggshells away.

Parenting Time

Whether your grandchildren are geographically close to or far away from the absent parent, it should be made very clear to them that whenever they are together, this parent is not a visitor in their lives. The parent is having his or her rightful parenting time with the children. That parent can participate with the children in whatever activities have been scheduled. Another possibility is to offer a choice between activities that the non-custodial parent has planned for the parenting time with the children and the ones scheduled by the primary custodial parent.

The most important thing for the other parent, once the parenting plan schedule of the custody periods is set, is to keep to it. The children are depending upon it. The children are going to stop planning on being with a parent who misses scheduled parenting times. They will begin to think that parent doesn't care enough to make the effort to see them.

Even if your grandchildren have been relocated from your child, there are effective ways to be with them. My grandsons were relocated a thousand miles away from their father. But he refuses to allow any distance to get in the way of his loving relationship with them. He traveled to their new location and stayed for one whole week just so he could be there for each child's first day of kindergarten. He knew that the first day of their school lives would never occur again. Regardless of the extra effort it takes, it is so important to be there for those special occasions.

My son knew just how much this meant to a child. His own father had missed his nursery school graduation. In the middle of a jury trial, his attorney father had asked for a recess so he could attend. The judge refused, saying, "You will have so many other graduations to attend in the years ahead." But with his father's death, there were no others. He missed them all, and there were many. I thought of that judge at each of my son's graduations, especially when I sat in Harvard Yard and watched him being awarded his doctorate. Each event is important to a child. No one knows if the chance will ever come again.

For the divorced father or mother, separated from the children during the other parent's parenting time, the Web cam inventor deserves a Nobel Prize for the greatest invention of the 21st century. The funny thing is that no one takes credit for its development. What is known is that it happened in a computer lab at the University of Cambridge in 1991. Someone wanted to watch a coffee pot from another room so he or she could know when the coffee was ready. For children of divorce and the parent who does not have primary custody, the inventors of the "Coffee Watcher," now known as the web cam, even in their anonymity, certainly qualify for the prize. Surely this is what Alfred Nobel meant in his will: "Prizes for those who confer the greatest benefit to mankind." It certainly has been of the greatest benefit to divorced mankind.

From someone's need for caffeine came an invention that allows my son to visually speak to his sons three times a week. He can tell them stories from his childhood, and they can share their favorite books with him. On Halloween he helped them count the candy in their trick-or-treat bags. When they don't feel like sitting in front of the camera, he finds ways of entertaining them so they will stick around. Several times they have had friends over, and my son just includes them in the web cam experience.

On his younger son's sixth birthday, he had a cake for him, and they blew out the candles together over the web cam. He then froze the cake and brought them pieces to share the next time he was with them. Not too tasty, but definitely thoughtful.

In order to remain a completely involved father, even from a distance, my son makes sure the school knows he is a hands-on parent, traveling to their school to meet each of their teachers each year whenever possible, or having conferences by phone when it is not; even sending faxes to school for each child with messages, pictures and cartoons so they know he is thinking of them. When his younger son turned five, he even arranged a surprise kindergarten birthday party, which his older brother was allowed to attend. A few hours later, the teacher sent pictures of the happy birthday boy that his dad and I could share.

When my son is able to travel to see his sons, he enjoys his 24/7 parenting time with them by moving his sons into a local hotel when he arrives. For the longer parenting time, they are at home with him on holidays and summer vacations. His sons even got to come with him to Beijing one summer when he was teaching a Chinese foreign studies program. For a determined parent, there is always a way.

Dating Again

For the parent who does not choose his or her spouse's replacement before the ink on the divorce decree is dry, it would be helpful if that parent is very open with the children about when he or she intends to start dating again. It might be best, however, to start preparing the children slowly, before adding a new relationship to the home. A parent needs to be very sensitive to the fact that children feel the loss of both parents when their parents start dating. Instead of sneaking around, it is better if the parent is honest with the children about his or her need to be with adult friends.

It can be helpful to the children if the parents discuss with them how they feel about their parents dating. It also might prove beneficial if the parents explain that they have to make their own decisions about whom they like, but that they will give the children opportunities to express an opinion and to work out any problems. All of this should occur before a parent considers remarriage.

This is not just important in the beginning stages of the divorce. Children need to be assured that no changes will ever be made to the status quo until the children have a chance to discuss it. This need really became clear four years after my son's divorce, when he was speaking with his sons on the web cam one weekend and introduced two boys who were visiting him with their parent. At the end of the conversation, my younger grandson asked his father, "Dad, are those boys living with you at your house now?" My son quickly assured him that they were just visiting and that he missed their not being there too. In case you are wondering, yes, that is the same grandson who, four years earlier, uttered the never-forgotten words, "Mommies and daddies should live in the same house."

When changes are being considered, however, it is best not to give children veto power over them, because that kind of power can be a disaster in the making. One divorced friend of mine says that every time she starts getting dressed for a date, one of her children gets some kind of malady to keep her at home. Letting a child control a parent's dating can cause that child great feelings of guilt. If the childish behavior prevents the parent from reestablishing a social life, the child will feel responsible when he or she reaches maturity and wants to establish a life separate from that parent.

One of the benefits of shared parenting time is that it gives each parent time to start dating when the children are with the other parent. It certainly saves on child care. For those divorced mothers whose ex-spouses are not around, time with a grandparent could work the same way. They can then wait to introduce the children to a potential new partner until the relationship becomes a little more serious, or even if plans are made to make it permanent.

If the children are introduced too early to the people in their parents' lives, they might get too attached, reprising the possibility of suffering loss over and over again. When there are teenage daughters in the divorced home, competition can arise between mother and daughters. As a daughter is adjusting to her sexuality, the mother needs to avoid any behavior that might even suggest a dating competition is going on.

New Spouse in the House

Hopefully, before attempting a new partnership or remarriage, your child will be well on the way to a successful divorce. Although it is recommended by many child psychologists that no new relationship is added to the divorced family for at least a year, many of those divorcing make plans to try again well before the divorce is finalized. Some are making plans even before a divorce is requested.

It is much harder for children to have to adjust to the loss of their father in the home, if at the same time they have to deal with their mother's trying to substitute a new man into the family too soon after the separation. If the parents did not share the real reason for the divorce with their children, this is when it will give them trouble. These same children will remember the real reason as they get older. They will remember whether their mother or father lied to them or told them the truth.

You don't have to be specific. Questions and answers that are sexual in nature can be avoided. But children will question another man in their mother's bed, or a woman in their father's. This will make their middle-of-the-night or early-morning snuggles seem unwelcome. Don't think they are too young to understand something is very wrong with that picture.

Before a parent announces his or her intention to remarry, it really helps to give the children a chance to get used to the parent's new partner. Be sure to include the children in any plans for a wedding and give them a role in the ceremony, whether they are big or small. Whatever they do, parents should not get remarried and then tell the children afterward. Most insulting of all to the children is getting married and keeping it a secret from them.

Without telling her children, one bride I heard about got married with her children sleeping in the next room. Of course, her children were dressed appropriately for the ceremony, as bride and groom took their vows in a pajama party wedding. The children's father was the one who was left to finally explain to them that their mother had gotten remarried and no longer shared their same last name.

Remarriage causes additional changes and problems to the divorced family structure. If your grandchildren feel they are not being included in the decision, they might reach out to discuss the changed situation with you. Allow your grandchildren to express their opinions of the changes in the home. This includes the new stepparent, even if it is not too complimentary. Encourage them to share with you what they don't like and what they think their parent could do to improve the situation, then help them to share that opinion with their parents.

It should be expected that your grandchildren can become frustrated by the changes they feel are being forced upon them. This is true especially if their order in the family becomes different due to the addition of step-siblings. The oldest child in the family who suddenly is forced to become a middle child will resent his or her displacement, just as the youngest child will resent becoming a middle child with the addition of a younger step- or half-sibling. When a parent remarries, your grandchildren will be reminded that that parent once said those same vows with their other parent. If Mom or Dad failed the first time, what are the chances of him or her making it a second or even a third time? If the children are old enough to understand the statistics regarding divorce, they will understand that their fears have merit.

In some cases it is not the first failure, and that fact should not be hidden from the children. Those inconvenient little family secrets seem to emerge at the most inconvenient times. A friend of mine asked his twelve-year-old son to retrieve a document from his desk. The son returned, quite confused, asking for an explanation. He had found a death certificate of an unknown man amongst the family papers. His father quickly explained that it was the death certificate of his son's mother's first husband. The son was so shocked that his father thought it was time he shared that he had also been married before.

One Parent Too Many

If your grandchildren want you to intercede for them regarding the new adult in their home, arrange a time for them to be able to sit down with their parents, either separately or together, to discuss the problems your grandchildren are having. You should not try to solve the problems yourself. Encourage your grandchildren to suggest to their parents how they could help make their adjustment easier.

One of the most common concerns that children have when a new adult figure is introduced into the home is the matter of control and discipline. Children want to make sure that any disciplining in this new family structure is only done by their own parent, not their parent's new partner. This is not an unreasonable concern, since children feel they already have two parents they are expected to obey. Three is one too many.

The other concern the children often have is being required to adapt to an additional set of values the new partner has introduced into the home. This could possibly include additional children, and it will require a balancing act as skilled as that of a professional juggler. The children might worry whether or not they are up to it. It isn't surprising that your grandchildren are going to expect each parent in the home to show favoritism to his or her own children.

Another way a grandparent can help to explain to their grandchildren what is happening in their homes is by explaining what all the new titles in their homes mean. If their mother remarried, she acquired a new name, but her children's names did not change. The mother's parents can also explain that they have acquired a new son-in-law. The children now have a stepfather in their home, and if this man has children, stepbrothers and/or stepsisters. If their father remarries, explain that his name never changes. It remains the same as his children's. And if they now have a stepmother in the home, her name has become the same as theirs. But if there are stepsiblings, their names will be different.

With this new spouse in the house, your grandchildren are going to constantly be asked to explain this extra authority figure. I witnessed my five-year-old grandson deal with this problem on my first trip to visit my grandchildren for their school's Grandparents' Day. I wasn't in my grandson's kindergarten class for more than three minutes when the little girl seated to my grandson's left looked at him and then up at my son standing in back of his chair and asked quizzically, "I thought your daddy was…" With that, I heard my grandson quickly interrupt her, replying emphatically, "This is my daddy!"

So Sorry

Whether either parent has remarried or not, accomplishing a successful divorce should be one of the main life goals of both parents. Sincere apologizing will help. How many parents, after reaching the decision to divorce, put their guilt to one side and say how truly sorry they are for asking their children to bear the heavy burden of divorce? And yet all children of divorce share this one common regret, indicating it would have made their burden just that much lighter if their parents had apologized. They would then know that their parents understood what they had asked of them. Even without an apology, children of divorce continue to ask for one gift from their divorced parents: that they work to achieve a successful divorce, one that can enable their parents to share together the blessings their marriage produced.

Rule Eight:
As Long As You Both Shall Live

Focusing on achieving a successful divorce is worth the effort for as long as you both shall live.

Rule Nine:

Sweeten Up the Lemon Tree

Grandparents are very special people. They come in different ages, sexes, and ethnicities, and they are found in every culture all over the world. Depending on their location, the importance of grandparents and their wisdom differs. They may not hold the place of honor at all family tables, but most grandchildren look up to their grandparents and remember forever their times and their conversations together.

Grandparents come with many pet names. My children called their grandmother "Amommy" and their grandfather "Boo Boo," and my grandchildren call me "Grandy," a name I chose for myself from a favorite novel. But whatever you are called, Grandmother, Nana, Omah, Granny Snooks, Glama or Grandpa, Papa, Grand-pops, etc., I hope you picked your name wisely, because it is what you will be called for the rest of your life and forevermore in family stories.

You have earned the title of grandparent when you have survived parenting your young, are still parenting your adult children, and are lucky enough to have been given the blessing of grandchildren. Grandparents are the glue that hold the generations together, the conduit through which past generations are connected to the ones that come after. There is something very empowering, especially to grandfathers, to know that they have succeeded in leaving the legacy of their fathers to continue well past them. It is a sort of guarantee of their own immortality.

Grandparent Families

Grandparent families come in many configurations: some in couples, grandmother and grandfather, not always sharing the same grandchildren. Some live alone, either widowed or divorced. Regardless of the grandparent family, both grandmothers and grandfathers are living longer. And as we live longer, we have more of a chance to be a grandparent, and along with our grandchildren, to enjoy it longer. With our very mobile population, grandparents may not be as geographically close as they once were. But with the advent of computer e-mail, web cams and cell phones, technically they are closer. Our grandchildren hopefully will be lucky enough to grow up with the unconditional love of at least one grandparent to sweeten up their lemon tree.

When I was born, I had one living grandmother, accessible only by a four-day train trip to the other side of the country. With the advent of WWII, train travel was limited, so I only saw my grandmother three times in my life and never really appreciated the advantage of being a grandchild. My children were much luckier; they had two loving grandparents and two great-grandparents who demonstrated to me what I had missed. My grandsons not only have three loving grandparents, they are also blessed with two great-grandparents on their mother's side who are so generous of heart. We will always think of them as part of our extended family.

Grandparents' Biggest Fear

In the beginning of the divorce, the biggest fear grandparents have is, how will the divorce interfere with their relationship with their grandchildren? I was especially concerned because my two grandsons were so young. In those early days all that went through my mind was that I would be separated from them forever, and that they would grow up away from their wonderful father. For a woman who had to watch her sons endure the loss of their own father in a plane crash, this seemed intolerable.

Once I accepted that the divorce was presenting me with the challenge of helping my grandchildren successfully survive this life-changing event, I understood it would help me to survive it too. Since I was so far away from them, though, it was going to take determination to continue my own relationship with my grandsons. But if I were successful, it would prove well worth all the effort. My son, I knew, had enough to contend with just dealing with the effects of the divorce on his children, without having to be concerned about my relationship with them as well. It would be solely up to me to define and retain my grandparent role. No one was going to do it for me.

Grandparents have played an important role in grandchildren's lives for generations. But as the world keeps changing, their role reflects those changes too. In the past, due to the life expectancy of grandfathers being shorter, grandmothers played the more prominent role with their grandchildren. Now that grandfathers are younger, healthier and living longer, the gender roles are beginning to blur. Grandfathers and grandmothers both consider being involved in their grandchildren's lives a top priority.

Reprising Their Parent Role

Once their child makes plans for divorce, grandparents are presented with a challenging opportunity. Their loving support can help their grandchildren adjust to the difficult changes that are about to be made in their lives. Now that more fathers and mothers are both working, and the ever-increasing divorce rate is affecting more families, grandchildren need nurturing by their grandparents more than ever before.

Some divorcing mothers find the maternal grandparents' offer of a welcome haven the solution to their economic and childcare concerns, at least in the beginning. Some grandparents make the move to their child's home instead. Now that more and more fathers are being awarded residential custody, the reverse is often true as well.

According to the 2000 U.S. Census, 6.1 million children live with a grandparent in the home. Four point five million grandchildren are actually being raised by their grandparents full time, 2.4 million of them after a divorce or a death in the family, or when an unwed mother is too overwhelmed by the responsibility. Of the 56 million grandparents living in the United States, 1.5 million grandmothers and 880,000 grandfathers are fully responsible for all their grandchildren's needs.

These grandparents are called on to reprise their parent role just when their burdens should ease. They put the "grand" in grandparent and are deserving of everyone's respect. My husband and his sister were lucky enough to have two wonderful grandparents who were willing to step up to the plate when their father, who had married four times, required it.

Whether living with their grandchildren or not, grandparents are in a good position to soften the negative impact of the family divorce. There are indications that grandchildren who have a close relationship with their grandfathers, in particular, have an increased chance of showing a more successful emotional, educational and social adjustment to their parents' divorce.

Grandparent Time

If your child has primary custody, you are more likely to be called on to help out. Your close relationship with your grandchildren will be able to continue without interruption. Ask your child what you could do to be helpful, like picking your grandchildren up from school or taking them to doctors' appointments or sports practice. Or suggest a regular grandparent's time each week.

If one or more of your grandchildren are still in the infant stage when your child gets a divorce, grandmothers may have the inside track of providing needed child care. Grandfathers would probably rather wait for the breast-feeding stage to be over. But they are always standing by in those early days, camera ready to capture every smile. Grandpa also might be the one to play chauffeur, either to take the older grandchildren to school or play dates, or to drive around the block at midnight to lull a fussy grandchild to sleep.

For older grandchildren, grandparents can prove to be the first line of defense. They can provide a safe, familiar place where the grandchildren always know a hug is waiting, somewhere they won't feel they are in the way or are letting someone down. Your grandchildren are seeking out a place where they can still be kids, a haven with someone who will treat them the same as always. They are seeking stability, consistency and continuity they can depend on in their earthquaking world. Grandparents should be relied on to provide undivided attention. Turn off all those inventions of the modern era; they really do get in the way of intimacy.

Just at a time when grandchildren need the most emotional support from their parents, they don't necessarily feel too comfortable going to them. They consider them unavailable, concentrating their attention on other things that are more important. This is where grandparents are needed to step in to act as confidants. They can give their grandchildren the emotional support, unconditional love, attention, security, respect, and most of all, reassurance that they need so much.

Children of divorce have expressed that they feel their grandparents are the only grown-ups that still have time for them. It isn't the quantity of time grandparents provide that really matters. Rather, it is the quality of the relationship established between them that they can always rely on. What is important to your grandchildren is that they have someone who is genuinely interested in their lives.

Once you have your emotions in check, there may be other things you can do. If you live close to your grandchildren, see if your child will give his or her approval to an offer from you to help the other parent too. If so, ask the other parent if it would be helpful for you to schedule some regular grandparent time with your grandchildren. Your goal is to develop a regular schedule with the other parent for you to see your grandchildren. To accomplish that, sensitivity is called for at all times. If you want to get time with your grandchildren, you need to leave your ego at the door. If you see your oldest grandchild overloaded with household responsibilities, like parenting his or her younger siblings while a parent is at work, offer your help for a time that will relieve some of these extra responsibilities.

If your offer of help is rejected, it might take a lot of diplomatic overtures and control of your dragon to make sure your close grandparent role continues. Ask instead for a convenient time, one that wouldn't interrupt the family routine, to call your grandchildren. If the answer is yes, don't get frustrated if sometimes when you call at the time agreed upon, the children aren't available or are not in the mood to talk. Remember, even little children have likes and plans of their own. Just keep calling at your scheduled time, but no other.

If you do get to say hello, don't expect long conversations. Just let "hi" and "goodbye" be enough. You might be lucky enough to throw in "I love you" too. If your grandchildren say they don't want to talk to you, don't take it personally. Each time, just send your love, and keep calling.

As a non-custodial grandparent, near or far, you might find the other parent unreceptive to all of your overtures. Don't be discouraged. You can still keep your relationship with your grandchildren going by taking every opportunity available when it's your child's parenting time. Hopefully there will be web cam time to make up for your frustrations. Also, children love mail. You can send cards and letters to them with stickers and candy thrown in. It may take extra work and challenges to be the involved grandparent you want to be. But that doesn't mean it is impossible.

Boundaries: Theirs and Yours

If you do offer to babysit, whether for your own child or the other parent, set boundaries to prevent your offer's being abused. If you don't, your improving relationship could be damaged. Give the other parent the opportunity to schedule plans that are convenient to you by providing a schedule of your availability, in writing, a week or a month in advance. The Parenting Plan Calendar is the perfect place to put it down.

Indicate that they can depend on you to help out with legitimate emergencies, with the emphasis on "legitimate." These would include illness, injury or death only, and yes, an occasional work-related issue, emphasis on "occasional." You can offer to be an emergency contact for the school if either parent can't be reached. Offer to pick up your grandchildren from school when their parent is in a bind, or arrange one specific day a week for you to pick up your grandchildren from school, taking them home for dinner and then bringing them back home at bedtime, bathed and pajama-ready for bed.

Even though you are a grandparent, you still have a life. Your time needs to be respected. If it is not, you will start to resent offering it, and that can only lead to problems. Grandparents busy with their own friends and activities are always more interesting to their grandchildren. It is an example to them that getting older doesn't have to be boring.

Your family boundaries need to be respected as well. This means never dropping by the other parent's house, or even your own child's house, without a call to find out if it is convenient. Always be considerate to the parents when scheduling time with your grandchildren. Don't get hurt or feel rejected if your grandchildren have other plans. When a time and date is set, ask your grandchildren if they have anything special they would like to do, maybe things their parents are not interested in doing or don't have the time to do. You could even make a list of the things they would like to do. Give each grandchild a turn choosing what he or she wants, so they all have something to look forward to doing with you. What you do with your grandchildren isn't what's important. It is that you think them important enough to want to be with and plan for, and that being with them is really priceless.

Be Prepared

When you get the chance to take care of your grandchildren, don't be surprised if their parent gives you a care do's-and-don'ts list. Even if you have cared for your grandchildren many times before the divorce, don't consider the parent's instructions as an insult to your ability or experience. It just may be an indication of the effects of the scrutiny the divorced parents have become subject to. They are proving how careful they are each time they turn over their children to someone else for childcare. Take the list as assistance, not criticism, something you are given to help make your time with your grandchildren easier by knowing what makes them happy and comfortable.

Whenever you are with your grandchildren, let "be prepared" be your motto. Always have an emergency list with you in your home and car that includes addresses and phone numbers for home, office, cell and e-mail for each parent, emergency contacts, and the children's pediatrician. Be sure to program your cell phone with the information too. In your wallet keep a copy of your grandchildren's medical insurance card with an undated medical authorization signed by one or both parents, giving you permission to approve medical attention for your grandchildren if their parents are unavailable. If you have never taken them to their doctor, make a dry run to make sure you know how to get there quickly.

Lastly, give a list to their parents with all the information they need to get in touch with you. Knowing you care that much will relieve any concern the parents have about the children when they are with you. It also might encourage them to agree to sleepovers at your house. If your grandchildren ever stay with you in a different city or state, be sure you have the information of a pediatrician in your area that will be willing to see your grandchildren on an emergency basis. Don't wait, like I did, until the emergency is at hand. Your regular doctor or friends can provide you with a referral.

When your grandchildren come to stay, or you are staying with them, try to keep to their usual routine. That's not saying you can't bend a little and be flexible. What else are grandparents for? But it is better not to let them get away with too much. Don't fall for that old line, "Mommy or Daddy always lets us have this or do that." You might think giving in will make them love you more. Instead, give their request the Parent Test. Did you let their parent do it, and if so, what was the result? Remember, testing the limits is what children do.

It will help keep you out of trouble if you support your child's methods of discipline when you are with your grandchildren, especially the parents' rules that pertain to your grandchildren's safety. It is also a nice idea to give your grandchildren household chores to do when they are with you. It will be just like flashing a sign that your grandchildren belong there and can feel at home.

Time to Share

Each time you spend with your grandchildren is a memory shared. It's a way to let them know they have a grandmother and/or grandfather who loves them and who will make time to be available to them to help them deal with stressful times. Grandmothers play many roles, interacting in wonderful ways that connect them to their grandchildren. For the youngest grandchildren, they are like a second mommy, or as my older son put it, his "Andmommy." This was eventually shortened to Amommy. Grandmothers love to hug, feed, bathe and rock their grandchildren to sleep. They often fill in for a mom or dad busy at work. Twenty-eight percent of preschoolers with employed mothers are cared for by their grandparents.

Grandmothers make wonderful teachers as well, since everything they do is soaked up by their fast-growing and fast-learning grandchildren. Most grandchildren have memories of their grandmother in the kitchen doing magical things that resulted in the most delightful smells. What grandchild doesn't remember a grandmother wrapping a towel around the child's waist, putting him or her on a stool to reach the counter, and giving the child the mixer blades to lick clean of icing, or using those special cookie cutters to create Grandma's cookies in hearts, stars and hands.

During trips to the market with her, grandchildren learned to sing special songs about the wheels that turned round and round, or "The Grand Old Flag" that flew high in front of buildings they passed on the way home. How many are reminded of their grandma, even after they are grown, every time they pick out a fresh fish or watermelon in the market and remember how she taught them the exact way to make the perfect choice? Some grandsons remember the fascination they developed with vacuum cleaners very early in their lives when their grandmas let them turn it on and off in order to get them over their fear of the noise.

Grandmothers can even teach horticulture to their young charges as their grandchildren learn how to help her in the garden. She can be a storyteller or a writer as she lets them type on the keys of her computer. My mother loved to paint, and she had a little easel, paints and brushes for her grandsons so they could paint beside her. To commemorate their first taste of lobster, she took home the claws and painted them with gold paint so they could remember the occasion always. No wonder granddaughters and grandsons remember their grandmothers with such special affection; they think there is absolutely nothing they can't do.

Lucky is the grandchild that has both a grandmother and grandfather. Grandfathers have their own special, magical role to play. Grandfathers love to make their grandchildren giggle from the very first, lifting their own child's offspring into the air to show them what it's like to fly. They can be their grandchildren's first magician as they watch their noses disappear between Grandpa's fingers or the pennies he makes appear behind their ears.

Some grandfathers teach their grandchildren to build things, letting them help build that dollhouse their granddaughter will never part with, or the treehouse their grandsons will never forget as the first really special place of their own. While a grandfather builds one of these future heirlooms, he will often have a small grandson by his side, each with a toolbox beside him: the old one the grandfather has had for many years, and the toy toolbox the grandson received as an early present. Many times when grandfathers dig in the dirt with their grandchildren, they are planting a tree that will give shade for their future play as they grow. My grandsons have early memories of their great-grandfather giving them their first ride on his tractor when they visited his farm.

The greatest thing that grandfathers have to give their grandchildren is their time. Time to fish on the shore of a lake or from a pier or boat. Time to look for little insects and turtles from a nearby pond, and then to create little creature habitats for their grandchildren to bring them home in. Grandfathers can teach about mechanical things. They patiently answer all those "Why?" questions grandchildren ask about how cars, trucks and planes work.

All grandfathers and grandchildren seem to share the love of all kinds of sports, with the grandfather cheering the loudest from the sidelines as soon as the grandchildren join a team. Grandfathers make great coaches and scorekeepers, and of course, along with grandmothers, are available to provide transportation to and from practice and games. It isn't so much what grandparents can do with their grandchildren that makes the difference. It is the love that is shown, the attention that is given, that makes the special grandparent memories.

Tête-à-Tête

Your grandchildren may feel you are easy to talk to because you are more likely to give them undivided attention. They can feel lonely and isolated if they are not allowed to express their feelings, so your giving them the opportunity to discuss anything with you can prove very helpful. Try to develop an individual relationship with each of your grandchildren that they will always remember and cherish.

On the day a grandparent's first grandchild is born, that grandparent is blessed with special gifts: two ears to listen, a loving warm heart to empathize, and two arms to embrace grandchildren in a safe and protective space. These special talents are definitely put to use when his or her child gets divorced. Two ears are enough for hearing, but for listening, grandparents use not just their ears, but their hearts as well. For grandchildren of every age, their ears are tuned in to hear the slightest of sounds, the softest of voices, the fewest of words, and the quietest of wishes.

To encourage conversations, talk to your grandchildren about things that are important to you, or perhaps topics they are discussing in school about the world. Share with them problems you are dealing with, like health, someone who hurts your feelings, or work you don't like, and ask them what they think you could do to solve them. It might help them to know that all people have problems. It might encourage them to share their problems with you. When you talk to them, engage in a two-way conversation, with lots of "I" messages. They will tune out if they perceive you are lecturing at them instead of interacting with them. The clue to a disconnect is those rolling eyes.

Talking may not be too easy in the beginning. Be alert to subtle signs. Be there when they want and need you. Retreat quickly when they ask you to back off. But always be ready to respond, so they know you have their real interests at heart. Try different approaches, like communicating without talking. They may be encouraged to get things off their chests when you are doing a homework project with them, driving to a sporting event, or just walking along with them at the neighborhood mall. That conversation might even begin when you sit by them reading a book, or give a back rub while they relax for sleep.

When your grandchildren feel safe enough to express their feelings about the family divorce, be prepared. Their expressions might be in words, in pictures, or in writing. Your grandchildren are looking for someone to talk to about personal family matters, things they will never be able to talk to their friends about. So let them know they can say absolutely anything to you without fear of your repeating it, unless they give you an O.K.

They need you to listen to what they have to say and know they have been heard. They are hoping you will reassure them that they have the right to feel the way they do, and you will not criticize or judge them for the way they are feeling, that you will understand. Whatever you do, don't be a "graminator," the grandparent who responds with "you shouldn't feel that way" or gives some other overly judgmental comment about what feelings would be more appropriate. Children want to be accepted, not judged.

Children's Solutions in an Adult World

Grandmothers and grandfathers listen to their grandchildren differently. Grandmothers are the more touchy-feely of the two. They are more able to empathize with the emotional pain their grandchildren are dealing with, worrying ahead about the emotional toll the divorce might inflict on them. Grandfathers seem to be ill-at-ease with anything dealing with feelings and emotions. They seem to be much more comfortable focusing on existing problems. Proceed with caution. You might be very tempted to solve each and every one of your grandchildren's problems as they present themselves. Instead, grandparents can give them the greatest gift of all: sharing the life coping skills you have learned.

A good starting place is with a problem they are actually experiencing. Explain to your grandchildren that there are always several alternative solutions to any problem that arises. These problems can develop at home, school, or anywhere else in their expanding world. Share with them that they can choose which solutions they want to suggest to their parents. Your job as grandparent is to teach them how that can be done.

First, give them several examples of ways you think the problem at hand can be solved. Then ask your grandchild to suggest ways he or she would like the problem to be handled. Second, discuss the pros and cons of each of your suggestions. But be sure to discourage the child from resorting to the parent guilt trip as one of the solutions. That choice is never productive. Then ask the child to write down his or her three favorite solutions (all of which he or she could live with). If the child can't write yet, let him or her dictate them to you. Explain that presenting solutions, preferably in writing, will make the decision easier for anyone the child needs to approach. That was one of the best things my late husband taught me, and I love to pass that on to his grandchildren.

The next step is for your grandchild to show the suggestions to his or her parents so they can discuss the solution to the problem together. But first you need to teach the child how to decide when the time is right. The trick to that is to learn how to read the red light, green light signals being displayed at home. Red Light (stop, don't approach) signals are the following: parent first walking in the door, frowning, speaking in an angry voice, talking on the phone, sibling crying. Green light (go ahead) signals are as follows: parent is smiling or laughing, speaking in soft voice, dinner and dishes are done and the child helped. Let your grandchildren know, before they approach their parents, that all their thought and preparation will pay off. It might even give them an advantage in any discussion.

I have found that one of the reasons people won't make decisions immediately is that they haven't been given the time to think up a solution themselves. The easiest first response to most requests is no. Be sure to tell your grandchildren the story about a former President of the United States who first answered no to any question presented to him. He found that it permitted him more time to review the options before he answered yes. He was known to say you could always change your mind when you said no, but never when you said yes.

The moral of the story is, if you want a decision to be in your favor, give the person making the decision acceptable options and time to think them out. So be sure to share with your grandchildren that they shouldn't push for a fast decision. Giving someone time to think over his or her answer is a great way of exhibiting maturity. This is a great secret to share with your teenage grandchildren.

The last thing is to advise your grandchildren to listen to their parents' problems too. Maybe some of them will be shared. If so, they could work with their parents to solve them together. With these lessons learned, your grandchildren will know the joy and pleasure of the feeling of empowerment. They will learn to solve problems for themselves, always knowing that if they need to stand up for themselves in a situation that is still a little beyond them, that you will be there to back them up. Your guidance can prove to be invaluable, and that will last a lifetime—your grandchildren's lifetimes, not yours.

Three "Never" Rules

There are three fundamental rules for all grandfathers and grandmothers to remember:

a. never go behind the parents' backs, doing something you are fully aware the parents would not approve of;

b. never agree to keep secrets from your child or the other parent; and

c. never badmouth the other parent in front of your grand-children.

Keep your opinions as positive as possible about both parents and their other grandparents. Speak as if everything you say is always being recorded, which it is—in your grandchildren's memory.

Let your grandchildren know they can discuss anything with you. But that doesn't mean that you have to agree with them. Make sure they understand that each of you is allowed to have a different opinion, without either of you being wrong or getting angry with the other. It also doesn't mean you are saying their parents were wrong, only that every person sees his or her own life and actions as they pertain to that person, and not necessarily how they affect others. Acknowledging that everyone makes mistakes in his or her life might help your grandchildren look at their parents' behavior in proper perspective. There also may be times when you agree with their parent's decision in a family conflict. So explain why, in some instances, you believe their parent to be correct.

Your grandchildren may tell you something that you feel needs to be discussed with your child. That doesn't mean you should offer messenger services. Remember what happens to the messenger. Instead, encourage your grandchildren to take that problem to their mom or dad. Once they do, you can be free to follow up with your child on your own.

There are times when you might observe a potential problem arising, a dangerous situation that one or more of your grandchildren are being exposed to. Don't remain silent! But first, discuss it with your grandchild. Let your grandchild know what your concerns are. Give him or her the chance to go to the parents before you do. Make sure you present any observed problems without criticism; otherwise you might run into defensive posturing, which is always unproductive. Advise them it is because you care so much for them that the problem you have observed must be discussed with their parents, and you intend to be there to help them.

A grandparent's sensitivity to potential problems is not unreasonable. Statistics show that higher rates of substance abuse, teenage pregnancy, depression, juvenile delinquency or even teenage suicide are often found among children of divorce. These problems are too serious to be ignored. The one thing grandparents of a divorced child must always be aware of is that they should never discuss any problems with the other parent of their grandchildren. That is the exclusive responsibility of their own child.

Passing the Truth Test

As time passes after the divorce, you will have to accept that tremendous changes have occurred in your grandchildren's lives. Adjusting to the divorce will not be easy on them. It doesn't help that these changes occur without much preparation. And what is worse, the changes often occur without any discussion about them between parent and child. If grandparents pretend nothing has changed, the grandchildren will consider them insincere. It seems to them like everything has changed.

Your grandchildren may see their grandmother or grandfather as the only person in their lives who hasn't changed. If things get too unbearable at home, grandparents become their "go to" people. If your grandchildren get the sense that something is being kept from them at home, it is very possible they may ask either their grandmother or grandfather to tell them what is going on. They want to know if they can depend on their grandparents to give them the correct information without filtering it. This may be the only chance you are given, so don't put off an answer by saying it is best to ask their parents. Your grandchildren will think that because you are avoiding their questions, things are much worse than you are telling them, or that something is wrong with them for asking the question.

Questions are the way your grandchildren are testing you to see how truthful you will be. It is like an attorney phase of their lives. They might even ask you a question they already know the answer to. Your grandchildren are depending on you to be trustworthy. It's a test you must pass.

You will find that your grandchildren observe everything. They hear everything, they see everything, and they will bring up the most inappropriate things at the most inappropriate times. They may be too young to really understand what they are observing. But they may ask for someone, usually a grandparent, to explain it to them honestly. Listen carefully to what they say. There may be an underlying unasked question they want the answer to.

Teenage Grandchildren

If you have teenage grandchildren, there will be special opportunities for you as grandparents to help. Make extra time available to them. The teenage years are stressful at best. Add the parents' divorce to all the hormone action already occurring, and the problems are compounded, especially with daughters who may feel competitive with a dating mother.

Even in a two-parent home, teenagers aren't always comfortable discussing their problems with their parents. While teenagers are developing their independence, a normal emotional separation begins to occur. The same separation doesn't seem to occur between grandparents and teenage grandchildren, so your grandchildren may feel much more comfortable talking over things with you. Granddaughters very often seek out their grandmothers to speak to. Grandsons often seek out their grandfathers.

Grandparents have a very important role to play in grandchildren's lives regardless of whether their parents are divorced or not. However, if the grandchildren are adjusting to a divorce, that role can prove even more significant. Once they realize that their grandparents are actually the parents of one of *their* parents, the stature of your grandparent role in the family will increase in their eyes. That is the time they will be more receptive to establishing a special relationship with you.

One of the best ways to develop that relationship is to schedule regular time to spend with your grandchildren when you focus all your attention on them. Not all grandparents live around the corner, or even in the same general area, but that doesn't mean a special relationship is not possible. Many are "airport grandparents" like me, the ones grandchildren come to pick up at the airport. Or they are "over the river and through the woods" grandparents, who require a long drive to get to. These long-distance grandparents are capable of close relationships too. But they don't come without a lot of creative effort.

Understanding the Grandparent Generation

Grandparents play a role in their grandchildren's lives that no one else can fill. With their shared genes, they can develop a special bond, giving their grandchildren an intimate understanding of aging. It also creates a special tolerance in children for senior citizens, and the knowledge that being with the older generation can be fun. Even your illnesses and disabilities can be fascinating to your grandchildren. The example you set on how you deal with these adversities teaches them how to deal with problems they might encounter during their own lives.

As long as you do not complain about your limitations, your grandchildren won't complain, or offer any pity, either. They will just accept you and work around these limitations. After all, a grandparent's cane can be a lot of fun. It can become a gun, a sword or a great retrieving device for something lost under their bed. Ever since they were little, my grandsons have called my cane "Boom Boom." A wheelchair can come in handy too, a great chariot ride at Disneyland when they are tired.

When they were old enough to notice, my grandsons started to complain about parking in a handicap space. I never did find out what that was all about. Finally, all complaints came to an end when we were caught in a terrible northeast snowstorm, and suddenly parking right next to the restaurant door looked pretty good to them. "Every time you see that sign, remember your Grandy loves you," I told them.

I never appreciated how well my grandsons understood the cause of my disability until one day in the car when they listened to someone announcing a local charity race. My older grandson, age eight, said, "Oh, that is like you, Grandy! When you had breast cancer." The way he said it, I knew he was proud of my being a cancer survivor.

Grancurator

One of the greatest contributions you can make to your family is by accepting the important role as curator of your family archives. Grandmothers and grandfathers share the role of family historian. You are your family's connection to your ancestors, a link to past generations and a contributor to what will be passed on. Grandfathers are really proficient at taking whatever opportunity presents itself to keep telling those family stories. Don't stop him, even when your child moans, "Not those stories again." Remember there are new ears listening, and what you tell them they will pass on. If Grandpa's memory is not the best, hopefully Grandma will step into the void and tell all the stories of their side of the grandchildren's family.

Every grandparent comes with memories of at least five generations: two behind them, their own parents and grandparents, and three generations forward—their own, plus their children and grandchildren, and sometimes even great-grandchildren. This connection allows grandparents to educate their offspring about the traditions in the family. Most folks have seen the commercial of the little girl watching her father eating a peanut butter sandwich, folding it just the way her grandfather did. In our family, it was peanut butter and banana sandwiches.

Your grandchildren might not be too interested in their ancestors when they are young. But they will be extremely interested as they grow older, suddenly thinking about leaving memories of their own. I always regretted never sitting down with my father and asking him more details about his childhood. It suddenly became so important to me after he died, and of course, then it was too late.

When my father died, among his things he left an old battered black tin box with a small red cross on the top. I had never seen it while he was alive. My mother explained that my father had never been willing to part with it. He considered it one of his most precious possessions. It used to contain his mother's insulin shot paraphernalia. My mother told me that, from the age of 14 to 17, my father had used it to administer his mother's insulin shots for her diabetic condition until she died. I was very touched. It also helped me explain the diabetes I have now.

If memories are not preserved in some way, all that is left when grandparents are gone are the physical similarities that pop up in future generations. Maybe those same Buddha-shaped ears or turned-up nose, or that special stealing from the cookie jar look that my father always had, and that I now see on my younger grandson's face. You and your parents will always be remembered by the memories you leave.

Families in the beginning of the 20th century were more interested in assimilating into the culture of the young country they had become part of than in remembering the one they had left behind. But by the beginning of the 21st century, the focus had changed. People have now become interested in capturing their past before it is too late. Perhaps it was the aging and dying of "The Greatest Generation," the subject of Tom Brokaw's book, that sparked the growing interest. Many of that generation, the veterans and survivors of WWII, are the grandparents of today.

Or possibly it was the creation by Steven Spielberg of the Survivors of the Shoah Visual History Foundation, the goal of which is to preserve the testimony of the survivors of the Holocaust before it is too late, and to eventually be able to disseminate these stories so this terrible period in human history will never be forgotten or repeated. "Technology and emotion go hand in hand," Spielberg said as memories were first videotaped and now are digitally recorded in cities around the world.

The success of the Shoah Project pointed out to more and more people that within every life, there is a story to tell. And the advancement in technology has made it easier to have people capture their personal histories. *Speak, Memory*, Vladimir Nabokov entitled his memoir. And now many options are available to enable you to give that gift of memory to those who come after you.

Courses like a friend of mine taught called "Writing Your Personal History" are offered at college continuing education departments all over the country. There are even courses available online. Titles may be different, but the goal is the same: to record those memories that you want your grandchildren to pass down to their families. Colleges are also offering language courses called "Language of Your Parents" so that the original family language won't be lost.

Continuing the trend, in 2003 National Public Radio developed one of the largest oral history projects of its kind called StoryCorps. In recording booths set up around the country, people are sitting down with a fellow family member or friend to record some of their favorite memories. A free CD of their interview is given to them, and a copy is sent to be preserved at the American Folklife Center at the Library of Congress.

If you want to write a living history of your memories, the Internet is a great place to check your options. There are also some helpful books in your library or bookstore. To record those memories, Grandpa, get out your voice recorder and start recording all the stories you and Grandma can remember. Or, if you need some help, check if StoryCorps is in an area near you. For grandparents who are intimidated by the job of curator, there are grandmother and grandfather memory books available at bookstores and online at AARP.com.

Grandchildren get a better understanding of their parents at their age by listening to your stories about how their parents acted when they were children. They especially enjoy stories about their parents' misadventures. It is hard for them to even imagine that their parents were ever their age, much less what they were like. Have you ever seen a grandmother or grandfather holding in laughter while his or her adult child, or the other parent, struggles to discipline a grandchild for something that parent used to be disciplined for? When you tell your child you know your grandchild is just like him or her, the usual response is, "I was never like that." That is the time to reinforce your child's memory and delight your grandchildren with one or two stories. Sharing those memories over time means a lot to both your child and grandchildren.

Albums of Remembrance

It is up to grandparents to keep the more detailed memories alive, continuing to create new good memories for as long as they can. Another option available is to gather all those pictures you have in drawers or in boxes somewhere in your home and make an album or scrapbook of your whole family history. Grandmothers are great for this project. They probably already have the albums they made when the parent of their grandchildren was a baby. By gathering the family pictures into chronological albums, you will be able to turn to just the right page, just the right picture, to match each story you share with your family. Above all, you are preserving one of your most precious possessions for prosperity. Have you ever listened to those sad stories on television of a family standing in front of their fire- or flood-ravaged home, and the reporter asks, "Were you able to save anything?" If so, the answer is always the same: "We saved our pets and our family photos. Everything else can be replaced."

When my mother died, I found a huge box filled with her whole life in pictures, including, of course, those from my childhood as well. When the family returned to my home after her funeral, my uncle, aunts and cousins sorted through the box of photos. Through tears and laughter they identified what pictures they could, recalling many family memories. Those pictures stayed in that box for another twelve years, still unorganized until fate intervened. On a visit to my grandsons I fell, broke both my ankles and was stuck in a wheelchair for three months. It was the perfect time to finally do something with the family pictures.

It turned out to be a major job, but one I will always cherish. I was walking again by its completion. I didn't know it would require all of the investigative skills I possessed. It was better than any crossword or jigsaw puzzle. It covered 136 years, from 1868 to 2004, and seven generations, a history lesson in dress and style. Most of the photos were still unidentified, but contained at least one relative I could recognize. I organized them first by decades. Then I organized each decade into years, each year by season, and finally, by matching clothing and background, which pictures were taken on the same day.

An album for my mother's family up to the year of my parents' marriage came first, followed by one for my dad. The year those pictures joined, I was watching my family begin. Those pictures were my past. And all the new pictures you are taking now will be your grandchildren's past, in the future. My only regret was that I had not sat down with my parents before they died. They could have told me the story behind each picture. I could never have anticipated the benefit of all that work. I found a part of my family that had been lost for forty years.

After my divorced sister remarried, due to many problems, we lost touch. All those pictures of my childhood made me determined to reunite with her and her children again. Having finally become more computer savvy over the years, I decided to attempt an Ancestor.com search. What a shock! I discovered my sister had died— not recently, but two months before my husband had died so many years ago. A copy of her death certificate led me to my oldest nephew, whom I used to babysit for when he was small. My son made the initial contact. Answering the phone a few hours later, I heard the voice on the other end say, "Aunt Jody, what took you so long?"

I was so thrilled that I had found him again, but I delayed our reunion for two weeks. I had something to do first. I had a gift for him that only I could give. When I found out my sister had died, I was anxious that one of her sons would have the pictures I had found of his mother to share with his brothers and my sister's five grandsons. When I finally met my nephew and his son, I presented him with an album of pictures depicting the first thirty years of his mother's life, including pictures of his mother, father and him as a little boy. It turned out he had no photos of his own.

My grandsons will never be out of pictures. I have albums for each, starting the day they were born. The memories of their early lives with both parents are intact. But the sad part is that since the divorce, the pictures in their albums only cover half of their lives, the half spent with their father. After your child's divorce, don't cut out the pictures of the other parent in the album. These pictures are to help your grandchildren remember their past, especially if they were very small at the time of the divorce. It may be the only way the children have of ever seeing affection expressed between their parents.

Tips on Collecting Your Memories

If you have pictures to organize like I did, seek out your relatives to help. It's perfect project for a family reunion or a picture party. It would be a great opportunity to get the family together. When your grandchildren come to visit, show them the pictures. Maybe they can help put the pictures you take during their visit in the album, too. Don't be disappointed if at first they don't appear too interested in looking at the pictures. There will be a time when they will want to see every one.

Grandparents can prove helpful after a divorce by creating a paper trail for your grandchildren. Put the pictures they make, the letters and cards they send, along with school programs from performances and sporting events, in their albums. Be sure you have them sign and date them, especially the artwork; those are their very own Picassos. Some grandmothers and grandfathers who want to leave a special gift for their grandchildren write letters to them on each of their birthdays, keeping them with the rest of the paper trail to give to them when they grow up and can appreciate them.

A few years ago, during a visit to my son, my grandsons were each demonstrating their newly learned writing skills. My older grandson wrote that I was his fun grandmother. My younger one, cookie jar expression evident, wrote that I was his worst grandmother. He then crumpled up the paper to throw it away. I smoothed it out and handed it back to him, asking him to sign and date it. He knew that meant I was going to put it in his scrapbook so it could be seen for generations to come. We had a good laugh over that one, and perhaps grew even closer.

Making these albums may direct you to other projects, like assembling a family tree, or an ancestor search of your own. Sometimes these coincide with your grandchildren's school projects, which you could work on together. There are so many things a grandparent can do. Who hasn't envied a granddaughter who was lucky enough to have a grandfather who made her a special dollhouse she has never parted with, or a grandson whose grandpa made him his first big bed in the shape of a boat? The memories a grandparent leaves are only limited by his or her own creativity.

I recently made a needlepoint pillow for each of my grandsons so they would have something of their late grandfather that demonstrated his sense of humor. He had once drawn a cartoon dog that he sent to his family when he was in Korea. I copied this and put it in the middle of each of their pillows. In the surrounding areas were things that related to each grandson. It was my way to bring the grandfather that they had never known closer to them.

Each Unique

Grandparents can perform a great service by helping their grandchildren identify their strengths and understand their uniqueness. They can give them support to help them accept their weaknesses, always working to help them build up their feelings of self-worth. Grandparents seem to have a special early talent detector for their grandchildren. They can do a lot to help nurture a budding singer, dancer, artist, drummer, writer, or scientist. Their help with lessons or summer camps might be just the thing to encourage those talents to develop. Grandparents can also teach their grandchildren to put those unwelcome naysayers in perspective, the ones who dash cold water on every personal dream and ambition. The ones with negative favorite words are the ones to ignore: "That will never work" or "That isn't possible."

I have always called those negative individuals "mayo men," because in China they reply *mei you*—my translation, "not possible." Naomi Levy, in her book *Hope Will Find You*, has coined the term "magdas" for those naysayers. "The world is full of magdas," Levy says, "who tell us what we'll never be, what we never can become." Grandparents are just perfect to teach their grandchildren how to remove the welcome mat when a magda comes to call.

Since the divorce, your grandchildren now live in two different homes. There they may be subject to different rules and traditions. It may be difficult for them to understand the necessity for such differences, but learning from you how your child was raised might help them understand. Grandfathers and grandmothers can share their religious beliefs with their grandchildren, as well as helping them understand other people's religions, especially if their parents do not practice the same religion.

Share stories with them of how religion was passed down to you by your parents, which holidays you observed, and what traditions you practiced during those holidays. You might also have to create new rituals and customs when needed, now that your grandchildren have to divide holidays between two households. It might create a happy memory to join with their mother or father to take them to the church or synagogue where their parents went when they were kids.

When my grandsons were born, I was known as the birthday grandmother because I made sure I was there for every birthday. After the divorce that was no longer possible, so we started a new tradition. When we are together, my son, grandsons and I celebrate half birthdays. It gives us a chance to always have a birthday celebration when we are together. I also send them cards and presents on the actual day and call to sing them the birthday song directly or leave it on the answering machine.

Any grandmother or grandfather can develop his or her own special memory. It might be singing special songs and reciting poems that were handed down to you from your grandparents or parents. Or it may be a special skill that was handed down to you, like cooking special family recipes, knitting or sewing, woodworking, playing a musical instrument, ice skating or skiing. You can even develop a special outing each year to commemorate each grandchild's birthday. I know of one grandfather who takes his granddaughter out for lunch and a shopping spree every birthday. Another took his granddaughter out for tea at a special place every year since she was three. One grandmother I know makes a special event every year when she takes her grandsons to see the fireworks and parade on the Fourth of July.

You may find that your grandchildren are going to seek you out to help them with their homework, especially if you are picking them up after school and staying with them in the afternoon until their parent gets home. They may need term paper ideas or help with a science project. What a great opportunity to pass on a little knowledge, and at the same time, you can praise them for how well they are doing. You can even instill a little thoughtfulness by helping your grandchildren make drawings or cards for their parents for those special occasions, since the other parent is no longer there to remind them.

In order for you to really understand what your grandchildren are studying and what is expected of them, plan a visit to each of your grandchildren's classes and talk to the teachers. It will give you the chance to educate yourself on what they are doing in school. It will amaze you how schools have changed since your children were in school, and even more since you were. Check on the school calendar at the beginning of the year so you are not dependent on either parent's informing you when school events, games and performances occur. Many schools have their calendars on their own website. It will keep those last-minute event bombs from being dropped on you, causing you to scurry around to change your plans so you can attend. Even if you are an airport grandparent, you can still keep up. Learn what subjects your grandchildren are studying. Send them any articles you find that pertain to a term paper or book report they are writing or regarding the author of a book.

Open yourself up to share in these events with your grandchildren's entire family, which means both parents in attendance and possibly both sets of grandparents too. When you show up, don't try to make the event and your attendance about you. Your grandchildren are the focus of these events. They deserve to have both sides of their family involved in the important times of their lives, celebrating their achievements together. You will find that your grandchildren appreciate your attending every event that you can.

If you live too far away and the trip is just too costly, either financially or physically, for you to be able to attend these events, send your grandchildren cards to express your regret at not being able to attend. Ask them to send you pictures so you won't miss out entirely. Knowing you wanted to be with them will mean a lot to them. Maybe you can plan your next trip to coincide with one of their games, school concerts or plays.

Cyber Grand

Growing up in the grandparents' generation, we became used to one-on-one communication. When we called customer service, we didn't have to press extra numbers or be directed by a machine. When we went to the bank, we weren't surprised to be greeted by name. And of course, we had that friendly milkman at our door in the morning. Today, if you want to keep in contact with your grandchildren, it is time to become a Cyber Grand—that is, a grandparent familiar with all the new technical advances, good or bad: cell phones, computers and, I must admit, God bless e-mail. Of course, you can still avoid using an ATM out of principle. I have. But I was thrilled the first time my seven-year-old grandson called me from his own phone to tell me my number was now added to his speed dial.

I hope you weren't like me when I went to purchase my first computer. I armed myself with a son on either arm, but that still didn't help. A salesman began with the pixels and megabytes, hard drives and software, and I ran screaming from the store. Oh, O.K. I didn't exactly yell out loud, but inside I was definitely screaming. It took awhile, but I finally had to face the fact that if I wanted to be an up-to-date grandmother in my grandchildren's computer-driven world, I would have to get a computer. I also have to admit I couldn't have written this book without it.

One of my best girlfriends fought the fight for a long time. She was a crossword puzzle fanatic, and I kept telling her she would absolutely love doing her puzzles with a computer available. Also, to tell the truth, I got tired of the phone calls asking me to look up all those crossword puzzle words. Her grandsons finally had enough of their computer-illiterate grandma, who in all other respects was the coolest grandmother on the planet. So last Christmas a computer, with red bow on top, was under her tree.

If you are still holding out, it is time to take the plunge. Being Internet savvy will definitely get you the respect of your grandchildren. I know it is scary, but being able to use a computer will broaden your horizons and give you the techniques to keep in touch with your grandchildren and a lot of old friends as well. There are computer classes for senior citizens at your local high school, senior center, library, or local computer store. There are even special computers designed especially for seniors, with larger keyboards and brighter screens. It is the perfect answer for the airport grandparent and disabled grandparent: an easy way to communicate with your grandchildren.

So be sure to ask your child, or the other parent, if your grandchildren have access to a computer. If they can't read your e-mails yet, ask the other parent to please pass on your messages. If you feel that your grandchildren aren't getting your messages, keep a copy of each one and then go over what they said when you are with them. If your grandchildren are old enough to use their own computer, but don't have one, that might be a great gift for you and their parent to join together to give them if it is financially feasible. Check with your grandchildren's school. Some schools have arrangements with the manufacturer who has supplied the school's computers to make computers available to students to purchase at a discount.

If you are close enough, let your grandchildren who have already mastered the computer teach you. They will get such giggles at your early attempts to learn their new world of communication, the new vocabulary of computer terms: downloading, spam, cookies, Googling. Also, they may have to answer that question, Why do you put a computer to sleep, anyway? Finally, they will be so proud of the way they helped you improve.

Airport grandparents get a great benefit from becoming computer literate. They can send weekly greetings to their grandchildren without having to interrupt them from their studies. Your grandchildren can access your e-mails when convenient. You can even be in touch if they are away at school or on vacation in another country. Until they are older, your grandchildren won't appreciate how much work it took for you to keep in touch with what was going on in their lives. But it will bring you joy in being able to communicate with them, even when they are young and not too enthusiastic about talking on the phone. Keeping in constant contact with your grandchildren will help you recognize the changes that are occurring in their lives between your visits.

One of the greatest benefits for airport grandparents who have learned to operate a computer is the invention of Skype and the web cam. It is the best way for you to reach out and almost touch somebody you love. I was able to watch my grandsons open up their Christmas presents, even though I was on the other side of the country. And last summer when they were with their father while he was teaching a foreign study program, I could even visit with them in China! The only problem I can see with the web cam is that I have to comb my hair and put on a little lipstick before I turn it on.

Becoming proficient with the computer is especially helpful if you are disabled, or you are no longer able to drive. You can keep up with your grandchildren's activities by receiving on the computer the latest photos and artwork and even copies of their report cards. My younger grandson was forced to evacuate his home during a hurricane just before his 6th birthday. On the day of his birthday he was surprised when he finally reached me. He found out I already had a picture of him opening up his presents on that very day, thanks to his mom. She had sent a photo on her computer to his dad, who then passed it on to me. A journey of 4,000 miles in seconds! Certainly an indication of a successful divorce in the making.

You can also be made aware of your grandchildren's latest passions, so you won't be tempted to send your grandsons Spiderman stickers if they have moved on to Star Wars, Ben 10, Bakugon or Avatar, or send your granddaughter Hannah Montana stickers when she is into iCarly. There are web sites that can help you learn what gifts are age appropriate, and then order them online. Of course, a check is always appreciated, but something thoughtfully selected by you can become a treasured possession.

All grandchildren love having a "cool" grandparent. Being able to communicate by computer is definitely a start in the right direction, especially if a picture of your grandchildren wallpapers your desktop. But there are other things you can do to keep that cool grandparent image going. Find out what each of your grandchildren is involved in, whether it be scouting, sports, ballet, music lessons, etc. Ask them if they have a secret wish. Maybe sending them to a summer camp devoted to their favorite sport or interest would be a great gift, or maybe they are interested in taking special lessons. If your child's child support budget is tight, grandparents can be a real help in funding some of those educational needs that crop up, like school uniforms, books, school supplies or class trips. If your grandchildren are of college age, there are always things they could use help with.

Maintain as much contact as you can with your grandchildren, whether in person, by phone, e-mail or letters. Not only can you send your grandchildren mail regularly, but if they are old enough to write you too, an appreciated gift might be some personalized stationery with stamps, especially those stamps you can have made by the U.S. Post Office with pictures of your grandchildren on them. Don't forget to include some self-addressed envelopes too. When you write to them, you can include some treats too, like little pops or stickers.

Special Gifts

Have you ever wondered about the old adage, "It's better to give than to receive"? Believe it or not, it is true. If you are good at keeping secrets, this one is for you. Start a secret bank account for each of your grandchildren that they will not get access to until they have reached 18 or 21, depending on the state where the account is located. All you need is a social security number for your grandchild.

It is also best if you put your child as trustee so it doesn't become part of your estate. A little amount each month can really add up. You know that big jar you grandfathers have been putting your extra change in for so many years? Savings accounts for your grandchildren are perfect for putting all those pennies back in circulation. You will get a lot of joy out of this project just imagining how surprised and delighted your grandchild will be when they finally receive it. They will realize how much you loved them and were thinking of them each time you made a deposit over the years they were growing up.

I was lucky enough to know how that felt because my maternal grandmother left a small amount of money when she died to each of her 18 grandchildren. I have never forgotten the generosity of that gift, especially because I knew what a sacrifice it had been. I know my grandchildren will appreciate it too.

One of the hardest things about the divorce is that I am not always kept up-to-date on the meaningful events in my grandsons' lives. I didn't find out about the loss of my oldest grandson's two front teeth until our next web cam visit when he was with his dad. Since I wanted to celebrate this important event, the next time I got to visit I handed him an envelope from the Tooth Fairy. I told him the Tooth Fairy had delivered it to my house in California by mistake. The note inside said, "From the Tooth Fairy for your two front teeth." Since I didn't want my younger grandson to feel left out, I gave him an envelope too; the note said, "From the Tooth Fairy. Waiting for your front teeth next year. Keep brushing every day." They were delighted, and I was quite pleased with myself.

That is, until my older grandson cuddled up to me and quietly said, "Grandy, why didn't I get a note last year, saying the Tooth Fairy was waiting for my two front teeth?" OOOPS! After suppressing a laugh and thinking up an appropriate Tooth Fairy response, I replied, "I think it's a new thing the Tooth Fairy has just started." The next thing we did was go to a toy store and let them spend their Tooth Fairy money.

The first time I got to see the space in my younger grandson's mouth was on the web cam too. He had gotten a visit from the "Mao Fairy" since his top front tooth had come out in Beijing. If you are wondering, yes, the Mao Fairy pays off in yuan.

Grandparents can also make a wonderful gift for your child and grandchildren by creating a calendar of different pictures of the parent and grandchildren for each month of the year. That way they can have those smiling faces keep them company while they look forward to the next time they can be together.

I know that most grandparents love to give clothes, and this might be the most helpful to a divorce-strapped budget. If you are giving clothes, make sure one item is a special piece of clothing. Boys like anything with the name of their favorite team on the front. Girls usually like anything pink. Ask your grandchild which piece of clothing they really want. If you are nearby, take them with you shopping. Your grandchildren are never too young to make their own selections.

If you love your role as memory makers and you are able to, plan a trip with your grandchildren, or if you are an airport grandparent, send plane tickets to your child and grandchildren to come out and visit you. A friend of mine has done something really special. Upon each of her grandchildren's graduation from high school, she takes him or her on a trip alone with her.

Don't give only gifts to your grandchildren that their parents have suggested. That doesn't really help develop memories. There is one rule, however, all grandparents must follow. Always ask the parent's permission for any gift that requires care and feeding or has safety concerns.

Just remember the message you are always trying to communicate to your grandchildren with everything you do. It is that you love them unconditionally and are interested in everything they do. Grandparents can play the greatest role by filling in where they see unanswered needs. Ultimately, the hope of all grandparents is that their grandchildren will remember they sweetened up their lemon tree.

A GRANDPARENT'S ODE

Life isn't always sweet, you know
Hence the lemon tree.
The bluebird is for happiness
Held so fleetingly.
With outstretched arms held wide
When life has reached an abysmal low,
Helping through the hardest times
With extra strength that's needed so.
Worth it all, my grandchildren dear,
They mean the world to me.
A Grandparent's love is a special thing,
That sweetens up the lemon tree.

—J. Rudelson

Rule Nine:
Sweeten Up the Lemon Tree

Add the sugar to your grandchildren's lives.
.
.

Rule Ten

Second Choice

There is a common wish shared by every child of divorce. It's either held silently in their hearts, or whispered softly in the darkness of the night, like my grandson did when he was only three. "Mommies and daddies should live in the same house." Although the first choice of all the children of divorce is for their parents to get back together, the reality of the situation is that most do not. For these children, from their view the best of the best is no longer available.

Marriages do not last as long as they used to. Waiting for the children to grow up is no longer the rule. Children of divorce are younger and younger, some too young to even remember when their parents lived with them in the same house. The memories may be vague, but regardless of their ages, the feeling of something missing in their lives remains. It may be painful, but you will have to recognize that from your grandchildren's perspective, their lives are no longer the best their parents can do, but sadly, only the best of adequate. Because the family divorce has the potential of inflicting the greatest harm on its weakest members, the focus of all the adults in the family, including the grandparents, has to be on minimizing damage to the children.

Best of Adequate

Once the future benefits of lightening the load for the children of divorce are recognized, all the effort will prove well worth it. There are many helpful things parents and grandparents can do to help the children adjust to the divorce in the family and assist them in leading healthier and happier adult lives. To achieve this goal to help our children of divorce, this grandmother suggests that the members of each divorced family join together in the following pledge:

THE DIVORCED FAMILY PLEDGE

To achieve the best of adequate for our children of divorce, we pledge for the children the following:

1. The right to love both parents equally, without pressure from either parent, of any kind, for any reason, to do otherwise.

2. The right to spend quality time with each parent, and for each parent to be flexible with that time where required.

3. The right to communicate with both parents, and all grandparents, at a time previously agreed to, by all means available, including telephone, answering machine, cell phone, computer, web cam, fax or mail, without any interference from either parent, and the right to keep all property resulting from such communication as their private property, without being released to any other person or entity without their permission.

4. The right, with their parents' knowledge and consent, to have their personal property carried with them from one of their homes to the other, including photographs of their parents, which they will be allowed to display without limitations in their rooms at both homes.

5. The right to be free of all negative comments or suggestive innuendos about a parent, parent's home or extended family, by the other parent or other grandparents.

6. The freedom from being lied to, and the right to expect and receive, in an age-appropriate manner, only the truth from both parents, grandparents, adult caretakers, and individuals in authority,

and to have no information withheld from them of any kind that directly affects them, regardless of their age or maturity.

7. The right to always be referred to and identified by their rightful name in all situations, regardless of the name currently being used by a parent or other adult in their home which differs from theirs. Along with this comes the right to be identified as the daughter or son of their natural or adoptive parent. Stepfathers or stepmothers may think they are helping their stepchildren to claim them as their own, but to these children, this misidentification only adds to the longing they have for their very own absent parent. "Step" is an accurate legal term, and it is not politically incorrect to use it.

8. The freedom from either parent, or any other individual, using the children as messengers.

9. The right to have an exclusive relationship with any or all of their living grandparents, without being forced to include any parent of a step-parent unless it is their wish to do so.

10. The right to be made aware of the details of the financial support being made by either parent to the children for their benefit, how it is used for their care, and if and when this support is ever withheld.

These rights would be a great start for any child to feel loved, supported and respected.

Joint Forces

One of the ways children judge their parents' genuine interest in their lives is how they conduct themselves after the divorce. In the beginning stages of the divorce, your grandchildren need and deserve to have almost one hundred percent of their parents' love and attention, as well as yours. Your grandchildren need you and their parents to acknowledge that their divorce has added an extra burden on them. It will prove so meaningful to your grandchildren to let them know how much their cooperation with all the changes in the family has been appreciated.

Your grandchildren will certainly find their load much lighter if they feel a great deal of love and support from both parents. Parents who have taken the "YOU" and the "ME" out of their divorce and have finally agreed to work together for the benefit of their children will certainly be adding to their children's feelings of security and stability. Additionally, if all the grandparents support this family effort, achieving a successful divorce will be possible.

Both parents and children will discover that it is not the quantity of time each parent spends with his or her child that matters. It is the quality and reliability of the relationship the parents establish with each other that is important, as well as how each parent relates to the other when they are together, especially around the children. This should serve to relieve any guilt that the non-custodial parent has for having less day-to-day time with his or her children. The involvement and interest that each parent and grandparent has in your grandchildren's lives will have the most minimizing effect on the damage inflicted by the divorce. There is also an additional benefit to be gained if all of the grandparents on both sides of your grandchildren's family work towards a positive relationship. Remember, your grandchildren can spot an insincere emotion a mile away, so always be real.

Problem-Solving People

If your grandchildren feel their parents, though divorced, are still on the same page as far as they are concerned, they will find it much easier to seek out their parents as the problem-solving people in their lives. Your grandchildren will be looking for that certain someone who is always available to listen and to discuss all the difficult situations that come up in their lives, not just the ones relating to the divorce. It is best, if possible, if that special person is either or both of their parents. There will be times, however, when your grandchildren might have a problem that they feel reluctant to share with their parents. The first choice of a confidant and advisor at such a time might be one of their grandparents, so be prepared.

If you are the one to step into the role of confidant, you will find your grandchildren much more receptive if you listen attentively first, and then in a non-judgmental way speak with them, not at them. Be sure your grandchildren understand that you expect them to be honest with you. Telling the truth, or hearing the truth, is not always easy for them. Your grandchildren are looking for some control over the things that are happening in their lives. Help them to develop suggestions to share with their parents that will help them gain the feeling of control they are seeking.

Expanding World

As your grandchildren's lives expand, they will also develop relationships with other adults in their lives, such as coaches, teachers, and those involved in extracurricular activities, as well as their friends' parents. It is a good idea, in this day of safety concerns for our children, that regardless of their title or position, parents or grandparents check these adults out. Once they have passed careful scrutiny, these relationships can be encouraged. They can prove to be excellent adult role models for your grandchildren, as well as a valuable resource for additional support for their parents.

Another influence in your grandchildren's lives as they grow older will be their friends. Children and their parents don't always have the same taste in friends. In fact, the choice of friends can be just the way your grandchildren will exert their independence as they grow older. For that reason, your grandchildren really need to be allowed to pick their own friends. Your grandchildren are going to benefit greatly by their parents' approval of their friends. It will indicate to them that their parents have trust in their ability to make good choices

Although a child's own choices of friends should be valued, parents might not approve of all of them. But a parent can have an influence on which relationships develop. They can encourage friendships with friends that they think are the best influence on their child's behavior. Don't forget, however, how you felt when you were their age and your parents kept introducing you to their best friends' geeky kids.

There may be times when your grandchildren will feel closer to their friends than their own family and will want to spend as much time with them as possible. Take that as a clue to include your grandchildren's friends in your plans, and they may want to spend more time with you as well. Even if you don't approve of some of your grandchildren's friends, being with them will be a way of getting to know what appeals to your grandchildren about them.

When your grandchildren are staying with you, make sure they keep you up to date on where they are going and how you can reach them, which is much easier in this day of the cell phone. Insist that all communication must be by phone directly and not by text. Meet your grandchild's friends and their parents too. A good way is to invite them over or plan a mutual outing, a good time to exchange address and phone information. Your grandchild might not feel too comfortable informing a friend, new or old, that his or her parents are divorced. So it might be helpful if you give the friend's parent that information. You might even find some of their friends' parents are going through a divorce themselves.

School Impact

Next to your grandchildren's two homes, the school has the greatest influence on their development. They spend approximately one fourth of the week with people, both peers and adults, who are totally separate from their families. It will be very helpful to your grandchildren if both of their parents actively get involved with their school. Even if they live some distance away, the parents can take an interest in what your grandchildren are studying. They should help where and when they can to make your grandchildren's time there successful. Both grandfather and grandmother can get involved too. Your grandchildren are going to love to know their grandparents attended PTA meetings or volunteered to serve food at their school carnival. If your grandchildren's school has a Dad's Club, grandfathers are always welcome.

Also, grandchildren love to know they always have a willing customer when they are selling something to raise money for their team sports. Almost every grandmother I know has a closet full of wrapping paper her grandchildren have sold to her for their fundraising causes. And grandfathers are pushovers for anything sweet.

The non-custodial parent who does not live close enough to attend all the school activities can get involved too. Wouldn't your grandchildren be delighted to know their absent parent felt they were important enough to make at least one visit to the school each year to familiarize himself or herself with what is going on, and so the children can introduce the parent to their teachers?

Both parents should make sure they make themselves available for individual parent-teacher conferences during the year, even if of necessity it is done by phone. But if one of them is not available for any reason, a grandparent who lives close by could play a willing stand-in. It is great if each parent and the grandparents, too, develop their own relationships with their children's teachers and have methods of communication with them, so the teachers can keep them informed about school activities during the school year, as well as any problems that develop. E-mail availability to both school and parents makes that communication so much easier these days. The non-custodial parent should make the school aware, at every opportunity, that he or she is a hands-on-parent, regardless of how far away the parent is located, and it is his or her desire, as much as possible, to be kept informed of what is going on in school.

Schools have become much more aware of how divorce has impacted their role and responsibilities to their students, so they usually are very receptive to the parents' need to be kept informed. If a teacher proves uncooperative, bring it up with the principal. Schools are also recognizing the desires of grandparents too, many celebrating Grandparents' Day so they can come and visit the school and classroom. Bring along your camera so you will have pictures for your grandchildren's scrapbook. This is one way to let your grandchildren know you are interested in everything they are doing. My grandsons sent self-made invitations to their last school's Grandparents' Day. Of course, they went right into their scrap-books. I couldn't attend, so I wrote them each a letter telling them how much I loved the invitation and how sorry I was I couldn't be there and why.

If your grandchildren, even with as much support as possible, show signs of inability to cope with the family divorce, encourage your child to get some professional help. Also, some schools have developed groups for students to meet with others who have lost a parent to death or divorce, so they won't feel all alone in what they are dealing with. If your grandchildren's school doesn't have such a program, you and their parents might work with the school to develop one.

Old Burdens

Referring to the problems of life, psychiatrist Carl Jung said, "They can never be solved, but only outgrown." It can be asked whether he had ever contemplated the problems of divorce. Children of divorce do not outgrow the pain they have experienced in their childhood; they just deal with it in different ways. The problems created by the divorce live on, and are more serious than most people think. How much damage the individual child has suffered may not be known until well into adulthood.

Adult children of divorce who have not gotten control of the emotional issues they have been carrying around since childhood will find additional problems added to their existing burden. They may want to develop good, lasting relationships, but find they have nothing in their lives to model them after except their parents' failed marriage. They may be so hell-bent on not making the same mistakes their parents made that they avoid the very things that can make them the happiest: love and family.

Adult children of divorce may find themselves avoiding or delaying commitment or marriage for a long time. They worry about subjecting any future offspring to the same type of childhood they experienced. What if their first choice is wrong? That fear might even prevent many of them from ever involving themselves in a long-term relationship.

Some adult children of divorce find that the damage they are left with from their parents' divorce is of their own making. They become frustrated and angry with their unrelieved hurt and end up acting out in very self-destructive ways. Unconsciously, they are looking for attention from their parents, positive or negative. Any attention, they believe, is better than no attention at all. It is known that children of single-parent families have a higher risk than those from two-parent families to become involved in drugs, truancy, promiscuity, violence, or criminal behavior. They don't consider that the results of acting out with such behavior will follow them for the rest of their lives. The sad thing is, the people they hurt most will end up being themselves.

Adult children of divorce can feel totally alone if their parents refuse to acknowledge that their children are still dealing with problems left over from the divorce. If in addition their friends are unsupportive, their feelings of loneliness intensify. The adult child of divorce is left with no one to acknowledge the lifetime damage the divorce has inflicted. And like they did when their parents first got divorced, they feel alone and different from those around them.

Lastly, adult children of divorce may be dealing with the alienation of one of their parents. It is at this time in their lives they will begin to question why that parent is absent from their lives. A sought-after reconciliation might result in two things: first, the affirmation of why their custodial parent acted to keep the other parent away; or second, the revelation that the absent parent was forced away. It is very difficult for an adult child of divorce to have to face that the problems they are dealing with because of the loss of a relationship with their absent parent were intentionally inflicted by the other parent.

If either of the parents has anything to feel guilty or sensitive about, this is the time to start working on changing the example they are setting for their children. There is always time to work on providing a new role model for their children to follow in the future, and still time to work on achieving a successful divorce even after one or both parents kept their dragons around too long.

Resolving the Unresolved

Some of your adult grandchildren will still be dealing with unresolved problems that have plagued them for years. They will find these problems preventing them from moving on in their lives. You may find they are looking for a way to finally discuss with their parents how they were hurt by their divorce. You'll discover they are seeking some recognition and apology from their parents for what they had to endure. Your encouragement might be just what they need to make that happen.

It is important to know that it is never too late for adult children of divorce to ask their parents to sit down together and have that conversation. And it is all right if the conversation is with one of their parents at a time. The parent needs to make sure the TV, computer, land and cell phones are off and put out of sight. No texting allowed. The key is to have the conversation without any expectations of perfection.

One of the benefits of such an open discussion is to find out how different the child's experience of the parents' divorce was from what the parents understood it to be. The parents get a chance to really understand the adults they have created. The children, on the other hand, get to understand, as adults, their parents' motivation for everything that occurred. In order for parents to fully accept what their adult child needs to share, they need to listen to what their child is really saying. They must learn the pain the child is expressing and how difficult it was for him or her as a child to experience.

Once these adult children know they have really been heard, they are finally open to discussing the past mistakes that they perceive their parents made, and to inquire whether their parents are willing to work on making their parent-child relationship better in the future. If both the parents and the adult children agree that focusing on the future will not be a denial of past wrongs, they can reach an understanding that they will work together so they don't repeat those wrongs in the future.

How Do We Handle the Parent Problem?

If by the time your grandchildren reach adulthood, the family has not been successful in damage control, their parents' divorce will continue to impact all the periods of their lives, and sometimes the lives of the generations that follow. When each of life's occasions, such as holidays, graduations, and weddings, initiates the "How do I handle the parent problem?" response, you will know there is still a lot of work to be done.

Will both parents be invited to graduations? At a daughter's wedding, will an absent father be asked to walk her down the aisle? Will he be asked to split the cost of the wedding? Will the mother be invited to a son or daughter's wedding when he or she was raised by the father? And if so, who will walk the mother down the aisle, and who will she sit with? Which parent will the adult child of divorce's family celebrate a family holiday with? After the child of divorce marries, there are four possible grandparents to consider. Who is called first when the first grandchild is born? Is the ex-spouse called when his or her ex is ill or has died? The parent problems can be endless in a family that has yet to achieve a successful divorce.

Divorce doesn't end till all members of the family are buried in the ground. Some families can continue to have problems all the way to the funeral of a divorced parent. One family I know even went so far as to publish dueling obituary notices in the paper, the natural children of the deceased and ex-wife listing themselves as the survivors in one, and the second surviving wife listing herself and her children as survivors in the other. The dueling obituaries were bad enough, but the dueling eulogies of the naturals vs. the steps at the funeral, each ignoring the pain of the other, took the funeral bad taste award.

Even with my husband's death, I was not spared the "What to do about the parent problem?" question. After my own husband's funeral, as the limo carrying my young sons and me pulled away from his burial site, I watched as the figure of a woman walked slowly toward his grave. I was shocked when I recognized the woman was my husband's mother, who had abandoned her son and his small sister so many years before. It was a painful reminder of the scars an unsuccessful divorce leaves on a family forever.

Many years later, when cleaning out papers in my husband's closet, I came upon the original copy of my husband's parents' divorce decree, dated 1943. It indicated the judge had granted the request of my husband, then a thirteen-year-old child, to live with his father and to take his sister with him. Unbeknownst to me, he had kept it almost thirty years amongst his most important papers. What I will never understand is, did he keep the papers because they acknowledged that, for the first time in his life, his wishes had been respected? Had keeping the papers protected him from ever having to live with his mother again, or did it represent the last time he did? Those will remain unanswered questions. I guess they meant as much to him as the black metal box my father left when he died.

Success in "Divorce 101"

What makes the difference with the divorces that succeed and those that fail? No magic formula is required. Any parent can succeed in "Divorce 101." It's really simple. It only requires two divorced parents who understand that their marriage may have failed, but who are both willing to take the "ME" and the "YOU" out of the divorce and work together to achieve a successful one. They acknowledge that in taking the action of getting divorced, they have done something that has put a great burden on their children. Because they accept the premise that their children's welfare is primary, both parents understand that it will take joint effort on their part, as well as all of the grandparents, to lighten this burden as much as possible.

Luckily, most parents see the benefits to their children of keeping a close relationship with the other parent and both sets of grandparents. They recognize how much strength children gain by knowing that both of their parents, and all of their grandparents, care enough to remain an important part of their lives. They are not alone.

Divorce doesn't have to destroy families as long as each of the members of a family commit to its success. The marriage may have failed. But if each family member always keeps focus on the goal of lightening the burdens the children of divorce are left to carry and minimizing the pain that remains, they will be on the road to achieving the best of adequate. Your grandchildren's first choice, the best of the best, may no longer be available. But with all your love for them, with all the family putting the children first, it can certainly help them achieve their second choice: All members of their family joining together, comfortably, to share and celebrate all the family milestones ahead.

Rule 10:
Second Choice

Always remember: It's not about you. It is *always* about them.

Bibliography & Suggested Reading

A

AARP Grandparents books

"AARP History." AARP.org

The Abolition of Marriage. Maggie Gallagher. Regnery Publishing, 1996

"Age Child Can Choose Where He Wants to Live." avvo.com

"The Age a Child Can Choose Where to Live." Martindale-Hubble @ Lawyers.com

"Alimony—The Basics (in California)." HandelontheLaw.com

Alpha Wives: The Trend and the Truth. Editors of *New York Times*, 1/24/10

"Angry Emotions—Your Child's and Yours." Elizabeth Pantley. In *Perfect Parenting: The Dictionary of 1000 Parenting Tips*, 1999

"Animal Mating Systems, Polygamy, Promiscuity, and Monogamy Trivia." library.com

"Are Your Kids at Risk?" Teri Morrison. *Divorce Magazine*, Vol.9

"At What Age Can a Child Choose?" S.P.A.R.C. (Separated Parenting Access & Resource Center)

B

"Benefits Quick Link Help for Grandparents." AARP.com

Between Two Worlds: The Inner Lives of Children of Divorce. Elizabeth Marquardt. Crown Books, 2005

Beyond Divorce Casualties: Reunifying the Alienated Family. Douglas Darnall, Ph.D. Taylor Trade Publishing, 2010

Bfstplk, Joe. "Lil Abner" by Al Capp, 1934-1977

"Block Bill to Protect Crime Victims Advances to Full Senate." *East County Magazine*, 6/16/10

"Bonding with Grandchildren." cbsnews.com, 12/10/02

"Both Sides Now." Brette McWhorter Sember, *Divorce Magazine*

"Breaking Up Is Easy to Do." Brian Willats, Michigan Family Forum

"Build a co-parenting team." s.help.org

C

"Calif. Bill Would Target Spouses Who Hire Hit Men." Cathy Bussewitz. Associated Press, 6/14/10

"Changing Your Name after Divorce." nolo.com legal service

"Children and Divorce: Helping Your Kids Cope with the Effects of Separation and Divorce." Jocelyn Block, M.A., Gina Kemp, M.A., Melinda Smith, M.A., and Jeanne Segal, Ph.D. helpguide.org

Civil Rights Act of 1964, Title VII 88

"Children's Bill Of Rights." Rob V. Robertson, Esq.

Collaborative Divorce: The Revolutionary New Way to Restructure Your Family, Resolve Legal Issues, and Move On with Your Life. Pauline H. Tesler & Peggy Thompson Collins. Living, 2006

"Collaborative Divorce: Developing Model of the Future." Mary Ann Aronsohn, MA, LMFT. nocourtdivorce.com

"Collaborative Law." Wikipedia.com, 2009

"Controlling Anger Before It Controls You." Psychology Association, 8/18/07

"The Co-parenting Relationship." Darlene Weyburne, BVD, CSW, C. *Divorce Magazine*

D

"Demographics and Family Composition 1992." www.ed. gov/pubs/YouthIndicators

Dinosaurs Divorce. Marc Brown. Little Brown Young Readers, 1988

"Digital L.A.: Shoah Project Becomes Reality for Spielberg, Holocaust Survivors." David Bloom, The Free Library by Farlex, 1998

"The Disengagement of Paternal Grandparents Subsequent to Divorce." E. Edward Kruk & B. Hal. *Journal of Divorce & Remarriage* 23(1/2) 131-147

"The Divorce Course." cbsnews.com, 8/23/07

"Divorce: A Problem to Be Solved, Not a Battle to Be Fought." Collaborative Divorce Training Institute

Divorce Casualties: Understanding Parental Alienation. Douglas Darnall, Ph.D. 2nd edition. Taylor Trade Publishing, 2008

Divorce: Does It Have to Be Destructive? Nancy J. Ross, LCSW

DivorceNet.com

"Divorce Rates and the Fault Requirement." Thomas B. Marvell. *Law and Society Review* 23 (1989)

"Divorce, the Financial Effects: Will Divorce Make You or Break You?" Catherine Dagger, beashrinernow.com, 2/9/10

"Divorce Statistics." Divorce Statistics Collection from Americans for Divorce Reform. www.divorceform.org/rates.html

"Divorce Statistics—Divorce rates 2002." Census Bureau Divorce Statistics. USAttorneyLegalServices.com

The Divorced Dad's Survival Book: How to Stay Connected with Your Kids. David Knox. Kermit Legget Books

E

Equal Pay Act of 1963. www.eeeoc.gov/policy/epa.html

Eagle Forum's Mission. eagleforum.org

"The Emerging 21st Century American Family." Tom W. Smith. GSS Social Change Report. National Opinion Research Center, Univ. of Chicago, 11/24/99

"Emotions in Children! How to Manage Them?" TheParent Zone.com, 7/14/2008

"An 'Ex' to Grind: Vile Gal Gets Jail in Bid to Split Kids, Dad." Kieran Crowley and Leonard Greene. *New York Post*, 6/11/10

F

"Fact Sheet on Divorce in America." Glenn T. Stanton, www.smartmarriages.com

"Family Communication." Positive Alternatives, Inc.

"Family Composition Changing." U.S. Census Bureau. Census Report 1995

"Family Law Is Biased Against Fathers." familylawsecrets.com, 5/28/06

Family Law Secrets Revealed, Fathers Edition

"Family Ties." Nicholas Long, Ph. D., and Rex Forehand. *Divorce Magazine*, Vol.9

Fathers and Families. Anita Gurian, Ph.D. NYU Child Study Center

"Father Facts" TM 5, National Fatherhood Initiative, fatherhood.org

"Fathers Facts for Features." U.S. Census Bureau, 6/12/2006

The Feminine Mystique. Betty Friedan. WW. Norton & Com-pany, 1963

"The Feminine Mystique." Wikipedia.com

"*The Feminine Mystique*: Summary and Study Guide." enotes. com, 2009

"51% of Women Are Now Living Without Spouse." Sam Roberts, *The New York Times*, 1/16/07

"Firebrand: Phyllis Schlafly and the Conservative Revolution." Elizabeth Kolbert, *The New Yorker*, 11/7/05

"Five Financial Basics for Single Parents." *Kiplinger's Personal Finance Magazine*. Kiplinger.com

"Florida Divorce Guide: Divorce Information and Resources for Families in Divorce Situation." StateofFlorida.com

For My Grandchild: A Grandmother's Gift of Memory. Lark Books, AARP, 2005

"40 Developmental Assets." Positive Alternatives, Inc.

"The Founding of NOW (National Organization for Women)."

"The Fractured Family." *UCLA Magazine* 7/10/06

From Madness to Mutiny—Why Mothers Are Running From the Family Courts—and What Can Be Done. Amy Neustein & Michael Lesher. Northeastern, 2005

From Your Grandfather: A Gift of Memory for My Grandchild. Lark Books, AARP, 2007

G

Gandhi, Mahatma quote. Thinkexist.com

"G.I. Bill History." United States Department of Veteran's Affairs

"Giving Gifts and Savings for Your Grandchildren." AARP, 4/9/07

"Goldilocks and the Three Bears," "The Three Bears" in the book *The Doctor* (1834) by Robert Southey

"A 'Good' Divorce? No." Elizabeth Marquardt, *Chicago Tribune*, 11/6/05

The Good Divorce: Keeping Your Marriage Together When Your Marriage Falls Apart. Constance R. Ahrons, Ph.D. Harper Paperback, 1995

"Grandfathers' Perceptions and Expectations of Relationships with Their Adult Grandchildren." Karen A. Roberto. *Virginia Polytechnic Institute and State University Journal of Family Issues*, 2001

"Grandfathers: An Untapped Resource." Fathers.com, 2007

The Grandmother Book: A Book about You for Your Grandchild. Andy & Susan Hilford. Andrews McMeel, 2008

"Grandpa: Be a Transmitter of Values." Fathers.com, 2007

Grandpa Rules. Michael Milligan. Skyhorse Publishing, 2008

"Grandparent Access Benefits Children Facts." Judy Atkinson. Cangrands National Kinship support, 1999

"Grandparent Contact May Help Kids Adjust to Divorce." Charnicia E. Huggins. stepfamily.asn, 4/28/05

"Grandparent Divorce Weakens Relationship with Grandchildren." Science Blog, 5/2000

The Grandparent Guide: The Definitive Guide to Coping with the Challenges of Modern Grandparenting. Arthur Kornhaber. McGraw Hill, 2002

Grandparenting: The Joys and Challenges. AARP Publications

"Grandparenting and Divorce." cbsnews.com, 11/26/02

"Grandparents, Are You 'With It'?" Justin Goodman. grandparenting.org

"Grandparents Facts for Features." U.S. Census Bureau, 9/10/06

"A Grandparent's Ode." Jolyn Rudelson, 2010

"Grandparents on the Other Side of Divorce." Kathleen Curtis Wilson. Grandparents.com 6/09

"Grandparents Raising Grandkids." cbsnews.com, 12/27/03

"Grandparents Taking on Day Care Role." cbsnews.com, 8/1/02

"The Grandparent Study 2002 Report." aarp.org

"Grandparent Visitation Rights Eyed." cbsnews.com, 4/15/05

The Greatest Generation. Tom Brokaw. Random House, 1998

H

Handbook for Grandfathers: How to be a Pal to Your Grandchildren. Conrad Veazey Brown. Writer's Showcase by Writer's Digest, 2000

"Helping Children Manage Their Emotions." Austin Child Guidance Center

"Helping Children Understand Emotions." Robert Hughes, Jr., Ph.D. MissouriFamilies.org, 5/12/2009

Helping Your Kids Cope with Divorce the Sandcastles Way. M. Gary Neuman. Crown, 1998

"Here's the Secret to Know When or If It's Time to Leave Your Marriage." Susie and Otto Collins. stayorgo.com

"History and Development of Collaborative Law." Nora Bushfield. iahl.org (International Alliance of Holistic Lawyers)

"The History behind the Equal Rights Amendment." Roberta W. Francis, Chair, ERA Task Force, National Council of Women's Organizations

Hope Will Find You: My Search for the Wisdom to Stop Waiting and Start Living. Naomi Levy. Harmony Books, 2010

"A House Divided." Elizabeth Enright. aarpmagazine.org, 7/2004

"How a Woman Should Prepare Herself for Divorce." Raj G. *Business & Finance*, 6/15/09

"How Grandparents Can Improve Your Child's Well-Being." Loren Stein. WebMD

"How to Not Get Screwed in a Dirty Divorce, Child Support, Custody or Family Law Fight." Anthony Comparetto, Esq., Florida

I

"If Not Ward Cleaver, Then Who?" Robert L. Griswold, *Journal of Women's History* 13:1 (Autumn 2001), Johns Hopkins Univ. Press

"The Impact of Divorce and Remarriage on Intergenerational Relationships." Dee Johnson, Essay 53473, mightystudents.com, 11/21/2008

"Infidelity Statistics 1992." National Opinion Research Center of the University of Chicago

"Infidelity—What Are the Consequences?" Marriage and Family Encyclopedia. http//family.jrank.org/pages 889/infidelity- what-are-consequences/

"The Influence of Grandparents and Stepgrandparents on Grandchildren." ext.nodak.edu, April 1996

"Intergenerational Relationships: Grandparents Raising Grand-children." Amy Cove. AARP Foundation Grandparent Informa-tion, 2/1/2006

"Interview: In Praise of Grandfathers." Dr. Robin Mann. Oxford Institute on Aging at Oxford University in London, England. *Aging Horizons Bulletin* 2/10

International Academy of Collaborative Professionals (IACP) www.collabgroup.com

"Is He 'The Loser' or Is He The Dad?" Teri Stoddard. Blogcritics.org, 2005

It's Not Your Fault, Koko Bear. Vicki Lansky. The Book Peddler, 1997

J

"Juggling Work and Family Responsibilities." Positive Alternatives, Inc.

"Just Grandfathers." grandparents.com

"Just Whom Is This Divorce 'Good' For?" Elizabeth Marquardt. *The Washington Post*, 2005

K

Keeping Your Grandkids Alive Till Their Ungrateful Parents Arrive. Walter Roark. Clearing Skies Press, 2004

kidsturn.com

Kids' Turn Central Children of Divorce

L

"Leaving a Lasting Legacy: For Grandfathers." Ken Canfield. Fathers.com, 4/25/07

"The Legacy of a Grandparent's Divorce: Consequences for Better Ties Between Grandparents and Grandchildren." Valarie King. *The Penn State Univ. Journal of Marriage and Family* 2/2005

"Linking Generations: How to Activate Your Father Power." Leland Griffin. Fathers.com, 4/28/07

"Long-Distance Grandparenting." grandparenting.org

"Longitudinal Study of Generations and Mental Health." Merril Silverstein, Ph.D. National Institute of Aging, USC Davis School of Gerontology

M

"Managing Anger." Jane Nahirny. *Divorce Magazine*

Marriage, A History: From Obedience to Intimacy, or How Love Conquered Marriage. Stephanie Coontz. Viking, 2005

"Marriage Wanes as American Families Enter New Century." University of Chicago News Office, 11/24/1999

Massachusetts Divorce Law—Law Section from GAL report filed 1/5/07 (removal) by Dave Goldman

Mommy's House and Daddy's House. Laura Kaufman. Trafford, 2004

Mom's House, Dad's House: Making Two Homes for Your Child. Isolina Ricci. Fireside, 1997

My Grandma Lives at the Airport. Rebecca Rudner. Red Hill PR, 2002

N

"Nabokov's Brightly Colored Wings of Memory." Jonathan Yardley. *Washington Post*, 5/28/04

"National Fatherhood Initiative 1994-2010." www.fatherhood. org

"National Grandparents' Day Originated in W.Va." Donald W. Wyatt. *Wonderful West Virginia* 9/95 www.grandparents-day. com/history

"The New Art of Alimony." Jennifer Levitz. *Life & Style*, 10/31/2009

"No-Fault Divorce." Wikipedia.org

No-Fight Divorce: Spend Less Money, Save Time, and Avoid Conflict Using Mediation. Brette McWhorter Sember, J.D. McGraw Hill, 2005

"Nobel Prize, History." Wikipedia.com

Nontraditional Families: A Guide for Parents. Jan Hare and Lizbeth A. Gray. Oregon State.

"Number of Stay-at-Home Dads Rising." Shauna Curphey. Womensenews.org, 7/4/2003

"Number, Timing, and Duration of Marriages and Divorce: 2002." Current Population Reports, U.S. Census Bureau

O

"100 Free Things to Do with Your Grandkids." grandparents.com

"100 Things You Can Teach Your Grandchildren." Stewart Coerver. www.grandparents.com, 7/21/09

"Overcoming Barriers to Grandfathering." Chuck Aycock. fathers.com, 4/28/07

P

"Parent Education and Family Stabilization Course"

"Parental Alienation" by Divorce Source

"Parental Alienation Syndrome: How to Detect It and What to Do about It." J. Michael Bone and Michael R. Walsh. innocentdads.org

"Parental Alienation Syndrome." Jayne A Major, Ph.D. DivorceMagazine.com, 2010

Parenting Calendar Software. sharedground.com

"Parenting Matters." Positive Alternatives, Inc.

"Parenting Plan." Eric Karlson, Divorce Coach

"Parenting Plan and Child Support Agreement." divorcecoachfordads.com/parenting plan.htm

"Parenting Plans Samples." sharedground.com

"The Perfect Divorce." Karen Winter. *Divorce Magazine*, Vol.9

"Philandering Animals, Fast Spins, Faster Circumnavigations." April Holladay. usatoday.com

"A Positive Divorce Resolution (PDR)." Positive Alternatives, Inc.

positiveparenting.com

"Postdivorce Relationships between Ex-spouses: The Roles of Attachment and Interpersonal Conflict." *Journal of Marriage and the Family* 53: 2/91

"Presumptive Joint Custody: The Agenda Behind the FR Rhetoric." Nick Seidenman. thelizlibrary.org

"The Psychology of the Grandparent Role Today." Megan Harrison. associatedcontent.com, 2/10/09

Q

"Queen's Golden Jubilee." ccfwebsite.com/news

Quote Lady's Quotes. quotelady.com

The Quotations Page

R

"Rebel Without a Cause or Effect: Birth Order and Social Attitude." Jeremy Freese, Brian Powell and Lala Carr Steelman. *American Sociological Review* JSTOR vol. 64, No. 2 (Apr. 1999), pp. 207-231

"Relative Power." Loren Stein. WebMD.com

"The Rise of Wives." Richard Frey and D'Vera Cohn. The Pew Research Center, Washington, D.C, 2010

S

Sandcastles™ Program, Inc. M. Gary Neuman

Saving Cee Cee Hunicutt. Beth Hoffman. Viking, 2010

Schlafly, Phyllis. Wikipedia.com

"Second-wave Feminism." Wikipedia.com

"Sidelining Fathers." Steven W. Mosher. Population Research Institute. LifeNews.com, 6/16/2008

"Single Mothers and Poverty: Agenda for Action." Report on the Status of Women in Montgomery County. Commission for Women 6/2007

"Single Parent Households Showed Little Variation Since 1994, Census Bureau Reports." Mike Bergman, Public Information Office, U.S. Census Bureau. 3/27/2007

"Skype: Definition & History." Wikipedia.com

"Slayer Rule." Wikipedia.com

"Sibling Rivalry in Step Families." *Parenting* www.thelaborof love.com

"Spielberg Recording Holocaust Testimony." Bernard Wein-raub. *The New York Times*, 11/10/94

"Steinam, Gloria." Wikipedia.com

"Stepparenting Dos and Don'ts." Jeffrey Cottrill. *Divorce Magazine*, Vol.9

Stolen Vows: The Illusion of No-Fault Divorce and the Rise of the American Divorce Industry. Stephen D. Landfield and Larry Cirignano. www.stolenvows.com

StoryCorps.com

T

"Taking Care of the Children." cbsnews.com, 8/23/07

"Taming Divorce-Related Anger." Anne Newton Walter. *Divorce Magazine*, Vol.9

"Teaching Your Child to Identify and Express Emotions." The Center on the Social and Emotional Foundations for Early Learning, Vanderbilt University.

"Top Ten Ways to Help Your Grandchild Through a Divorce." Dr. Lois V. Nightingale. Divorcewizards.com

"The Trojan Room Coffee Pot, A (non-technical) Biography." Quentin Stafford-Fraser. Coffee Pot Time-line 5/95

"12 Games To Play While You Wait." Jennifer Ching. grandparents.com 7/09

"The Twelve Rules of Grandparenting: A New Look at Tradional Roles and How to Break Them." Susan Kettmann

"Twenty-Five Tips for Parents Whose Children are Getting a Divorce." Laura Johnson. Chiff.com

Two Homes. Claire Masurel. Candlewick, 2003

"The Wage Gap: A History of Pay Inequity and the Equal Pay Act." Borgna Brunner. Part of Family Education Network published by Pearson Education Publishing as Infoplease 2009

U

"UCLA Course Teaches High School Students Language of Their Parents, Grandparents." Adolfo Guzman-Lopez. VOANews. Com, 7/28/2009

The Unexpected Legacy of Divorce. Judith Wallerstein, Julia M. Lewis and Sandra Blakeslee. Hyperion, 2001

"United States Number, Timing, and Duration of Marriages and Divorces: 2001" (issued February 2005)

U.S. Census Bureau Report 2000

U.S. Divorce Statistics (2002). divorcemagazine.com

V

"Vow For Now: Harmful Effects Of No-Fault Divorce." Robert L. Plunket. *National Review,* 05/29/95

W

Was It the Chocolate Pudding? A Story for Little Kids about Divorce. Sandra Lewis. American Psychological Assoc., 2005

The Way They Were: Dealing with Your Parents' Divorce After a Lifetime of Marriage. Brooke Lea Foster. Three Rivers Press, 2006

"Webcam 1991, Cambridge University." Wikipedia.com

"Webcam: Definition and history." Wikipedia.com

"What Are Grandparents' Rights?" cbsnews.com, 5/21/03

"What Grandkids Remember." Kathleen Curtis Wilson. www. grandparents.com, 9/22/09

"What is Collaborative Law?" Collaborativedivorce.com

"What is the Best Time to Divorce?" Judith Wallerstein, *Divorce Magazine*, Vol.9

"Why Divorce Rates Increased." Divorce Statistics Collection from Americans for Divorce Reform

Workforce 2020: Work and Workers in the 21ˢᵗ Century. Richard W. Judy and Carol D'Amico. Hudson Institute, 1997

"Writing Your Personal History" course. Robert Middlemiss

XYZ

"Young Children Often Misinformed About Divorce." Gay Frankenfield, RN. WebMd Medical News

Your Child's Divorce. Marsha Temlock, MA. Impact Publishers, 2006

Index

A

F

G

P

Q

R

S

U

V

WXYZ

CPSIA information can be obtained at www.ICGtesting.com
Printed in the USA
BVOW081306170113

310872BV00002B/244/P